Acts of Courage

Acts of Courage

**17 Heroes Who Won the
Cross of Valour**

John Melady

First edition title: *Cross of Valour*

Scholastic Canada Ltd.

Scholastic Canada Ltd.
123 Newkirk Road, Richmond Hill, Ontario, Canada L4C 3G5

Scholastic Inc.
555 Broadway, New York, NY 10012, USA

Scholastic Australia Pty Limited
PO Box 579, Gosford, NSW 2250, Australia

Scholastic New Zealand Limited
Private Bag 94407, Greenmount, Auckland, New Zealand

Scholastic Ltd.
Villiers House, Clarendon Avenue, Leamington Spa,
Warwickshire CV32 5PR, UK

Canadian Cataloguing in Publication Data
Melady, John
Acts of courage

Rev. and updated.
First ed. published under title: Cross of Valour.
ISBN 0-590-12449-8

1. Cross of Valour — Juvenile literature. 2. Heroes — Canada —
Juvenile literature. 3. Women heroes — Canada — Juvenile
literature. I. Title. II. Title: Cross of Valour.
CR6257.C76M44 1998   j920.071   C97-932123-9

5 4 3 2 1   Printed in Canada   8 9/9 0 1 2 /0

This book is for my grandchildren, all of whom are heroes in my eyes
— J.M.

I would like to thank several people who made my writing task easier, and who must share whatever tribute this little volume may deserve. In addition to the Cross of Valour winners themselves, and to others who are actually named in the book, I am indebted to the following: Bruce Beatty, Roy Bonisteel, Butch Boucher, David Boyd, Mary Bracey, Christopher Brooks, Robert Butt, Maureen Curow, Maureen Curtis, Jim Dean, Al Ditter, Bill Dunphy, Cliff Fielding, Robert Hughes, David John, Scott Larmon, Terry Leeder, James Leitch, Greg Mackenzie, Sheila Mackey, Kevin Manion, Rick Olsson, Kate Padam, Bob Patrick, Steve Rowland, Brian Salt, Dave Saunders, Arthur Schwartz, Paul Stanway, John Ward and Joe Williams.

I also owe a special thanks to Mary de Bellefeuille-Percy, Danielle Dougall and Andrée Traversy, all of whom were so helpful during my inquiries at Rideau Hall, and to Esther Parry for her editorial and word-processing skills. At Scholastic Canada, Sandra Bogart Johnston, Diane Kerner and Laura Peetoom worked to make this book what it is. I am indebted to all.

John Melady
Brighton, Ontario
November, 1997

CONTENTS

Some time ago, I was on a plane over the Pacific Ocean, somewhere between Tokyo and Vancouver. The flight was long and tiring and the magazine I was reading was not particularly interesting. But just as I was about to set it aside, I noticed a brief story about a man who had won the Cross of Valour, Canada's highest award for bravery. I was fascinated by what I read.

At the time, I knew almost nothing about the award. Later on, when I learned there was almost no information available about the heroes who had received it, I decided to write this book. In the process, I feel I have come to know a truly select group of human beings.

Foreword

At 11:29 A.M., the television lights came on, the military band began to play, and the crowd fell still. One minute later, the Governor General of Canada entered the room. He moved directly to the dais, smiled at the audience, and stood at attention for "God Save the Queen." Then, as the strains of the anthem faded, the Investiture of Canadian decorations for bravery began.

Heroism has always commanded admiration and respect. People who risk their lives to save or protect others defy the instinct of self-preservation, and in doing so, they show a generosity of spirit that is an inspiration to all. Such service and sacrifice should be celebrated. The awarding of medals is one way of expressing a nation's gratitude toward and high esteem for its heroes.

In 1972 the Government of Canada created a series of three decorations intended to recognize and honour individuals who perform outstanding acts of heroism. Presented by the Governor General on behalf of the Queen, these medals are called the Cross of Valour, the Star of Courage and the Medal of Bravery.

The most prestigious decoration of all, the Cross of Valour, is given for acts of the most conspicuous courage in circumstances of extreme peril. To date, only seventeen people have received the award. This book tells their stories.

Doug Fader

"If I wait, it's too late . . . "

He did not know it, but Doug Fader's leather jacket would help save his life.

Even though it was only the 27th of August, it was already cool in Fort McMurray. That was why Fader had worn his leather jacket when he biked to work. In northern Alberta, autumn comes early.

"I also had a new bike," he admits with a chuckle, "and I wanted to use it as much as I could before winter. Something like a kid with a new toy, I guess."

Doug Fader had been a radar technician in the Canadian Air Force. Born in Caledonia, Nova Scotia, he lived and worked in several places, both in his home province, in Ontario and in Alberta. When he left the military, his technical expertise landed him a job with the Alberta Government Telephone Company (commonly known as AGT), first in Red Deer, then in Fort McMurray.

When he arrived at work that morning in 1993, Fader learned that there was a mechanical problem at Birch Mountain, one of the company's remote communications sites some 120 kilometres away.

Fader agreed to fly there, repair whatever was wrong, and fly back. He had often done so in the past. One of the pilots from a local company would do the flying.

"Birch Mountain is really not a mountain as such," Fader explains. "It's just the end of a long line of hills that come through there. Most of the area is flat, with a lot of swamp, muskeg and scrub trees. It's more or less the middle of nowhere.

"Our company has a microwave tower on the highest point, and a hundred metres or so away the Alberta Forestry folks have a lookout tower. They have someone there all the time if the threat of forest fire is high, but there was no one when I went in. Our tower is seventy-seven metres high and the ranger one about half that."

Fader was forty-three years old, and the father of a nineteen-year-old daughter, Lisa. After his wife's death in 1991, his good friend Sandra Campbell had come into his life. All three lived in Fort McMurray. Both Lisa and Sandra knew that even though Doug might report to work locally, he often went to solve problems elsewhere. The fact that he was out of town that August Friday was not at all unusual.

It took about three quarters of an hour by helicopter to fly to Birch Mountain. The location is northwest of Fort McMurray, just over 100 kilometres from the Lake Athabasca community of Fort Chipewyan. There is not much at the remote site: the towers, a little forestry building containing a bedroom and kitchenette, and a handful of small structures. One of them houses diesel generators. Because there is no commercial power at the place, these run all the time; if one quits, a backup cuts in.

Fader would spend his time repairing one that had stopped.

"I never minded going in there," he says. "It was quiet and no one disturbed you. The job that day took me well into the afternoon though. About an hour before I expected to finish, I called for my ride."

When Doug Fader headed out by helicopter to Birch Mountain, he thought the mechanical problem he had to solve would require just a routine call.

Back in Fort McMurray, pilot Todd McCormack, a twenty-nine-year-old seasoned veteran on helicopters, left to fetch Fader. The chopper he flew was a red, white and blue Aerospatiale AS 350B, commonly called an A Star, owned by Canadian Helicopters. AGT used this firm for much of their contract work, and McCormack and Fader knew each other.

Shortly before 4:30 that afternoon, as Fader was gathering up his tools, he heard the A Star approaching. The weather was good, though there were occasional gusts of wind from the north. He felt that they would be back in town in good time.

As he neared the microwave site, McCormack noted where he would land — the same location he had used many times before, a grass-covered clearing about thirty metres south of the main tower and fairly close to the AGT buildings. His landing was without incident.

As soon as the rotors stopped turning, McCormack climbed out, stretched and helped Fader load the equipment he was taking out. The loading took little time. When it was done, both men climbed into the cockpit, secured the doors and fastened their seat belts — lap and over-the-shoulder straps that slid into a circular buckle at the front. They were ready to go.

The A Star is a versatile, single-engine helicopter, designed to carry a pilot and five passengers, or an equivalent cargo load. It has two rotors: the main one, almost eleven metres long, is over the cabin, and the second is at the tail. It is 1.8 metres long, and spins vertically. At the time Fader and McCormack took off, there were about 300 litres of aviation gasoline on board.

Todd McCormack made a quick visual sweep of the instruments before him, the engine roared into life, and the chopper lifted into the air.

For the last time.

Suddenly, just as McCormack started to make what is called a pedal turn away from the site, a brisk gust of north wind caught the aircraft. The effect was catastrophic.

The wind threw the chopper backward into a

cluster of heavy steel cables anchoring one corner of the AGT communications tower. The cables were taut, about four centimetres thick, running from near the top of the tower to their anchors some distance from the base. When the tail rotor hit the cables, it cut through three of the four, completely destroyed the helicopter tail assembly, and sent the aircraft into a sickening, sidelong plunge to earth.

Bits and pieces of severed rotor tore from the crippled craft. The engine shrieked out of control, and the machine hit the ground, right side up, 100 metres from the top of the hill.

"At the moment we hit, neither Todd nor I could quite understand what had happened," Fader told me, "but we were both alive. Both of us were still in our seats, the belts held, and as far as I know, we were both conscious. I remember thinking that we had to get out of there fast."

In what seems to have been almost a reflex action, Fader unhooked his seat belt, kicked open the left cabin door and somehow stumbled through thick underbrush away from the wreck.

Despite what he had just been through, he was not hurt in any way. Fortunately, the one uncut tower cable had held, preventing the huge red-and-grey steel tower from toppling onto the broken aircraft and the two men inside it.

Then the helicopter erupted into a ball of fire.

"I got a short distance away," Fader explains, "and until then, there had been no fire. But when I looked back, the plane was burning, and I could see Todd sitting there. He didn't seem to be trying to get out, even though there were flames all around him.

"I know there are some things that happened that

day that I have forgotten, and I suppose that is just as well, but I will never forget seeing Todd in the fire. I yelled and yelled at him to get out, but he didn't move."

It is at this point that Fader's courage can only be described as incredible. He was out of the plane, out of danger, completely healthy, and safe from the roaring flames.

But in those flames was a fellow human being.

"I remember thinking, if I wait, it's too late," Fader continues. "I knew if I didn't do something, he would be dead in a couple of minutes. So I went back. . . . "

McCormack still sat at the controls of the plane. His feet were free, but one arm was broken, he was in shock and his seat belt was buckled.

Because the right-hand side of the fuselage — the pilot's side — was wedged against a tree, Fader climbed through the passenger door and somehow managed to get Todd's seat belt off. Then, completely ignoring the terrible flames that were attacking his own face, hands and arms as he worked, he tried to drag the young pilot out of the cockpit. Yet Todd was still stuck; the burnt skin of his left hand had fused to the aircraft control column. Fader wrenched it free.

"When I got him out, he could walk, but I had to help him," Fader explains. "I knew he was in a lot of pain with his hand and his broken arm.

"I still felt fine myself, so we climbed up through the brush to the top of the hill. I didn't remember the direction, other than I knew it had to be up. I'm not sure how we found the building where the phone was.

"When we got to the door, I still did not feel too bad. But Todd didn't seem to want to look at me so I figured I must have been burned more than I thought. I had a big ring of keys in my pocket, and I was able to find the right one and get the door open. I left the keys in the door because it was the only way in or out and I figured whoever came for us would need them."

Fader then dialed 9-1-1.

His call was answered in Fort McMurray, and almost immediately patched through to Fader's office. His boss, a man named Al Forbes, picked up the phone. Then he, along with a colleague, Rob Pagacz, talked to Fader for almost an hour.

Meanwhile, a rescue helicopter was fired up at the Fort McMurray airport, two paramedics were rushed there, and the chopper took off. The time was exactly 5:10 P.M.

"I talked to Al and Rob and the 9-1-1 operator for a long time," says Fader, "and after I told them what had happened, we talked about all kinds of things. I had trouble breathing, and after awhile I felt really tired. They kept me talking though, and I guess that was good."

The conversation covered everything from Fader's time in the military to his new bike. Initially, to those keeping him talking, he sounded strong. But as the minutes crept past, he became less and less coherent.

"I remember when I was talking to Al I told him that my coat was bothering me," Fader explains. "I guess my skin had melted onto it, and the leather was getting really hard. He told me to take it off in case it shrank on me. So I took it off, and I remember when I dropped it, it just stood up on the floor. I guess it was good that I got it off when I did because it might have caused other problems later."

But it is difficult to imagine what "other problems" there could have been. There were third-degree burns to Fader's entire head, face, neck, hands and forearms. Later on, though he didn't even know there were such things as fourth-degree burns, he found out in the hospital that he had them. But the vital chest area was relatively clear. The black leather jacket that he had put on that morning to protect him from the cold had ended up saving him from heat.

The rescue chopper brought paramedics Rob Burke and Cam Sonnenberg to the scene, along with Don Cleveland, the Fort McMurray Base Manager for Canadian Helicopters. They saw Todd McCormack sitting outside the communications building when they arrived. The paramedics had been told that both victims had been able to walk up the hill, and were not expecting what they saw when they went inside to get Fader. They were appalled. One glance told them his condition was critical, and that, unless they got him to the best medical facility possible, his chances of survival were awfully slim. They were particularly concerned with his facial burns, because these were affecting his breathing.

"I remember the paramedics coming in," Fader says, "but I don't remember much after that. I guess they did what they could, and then loaded me up with morphine before we flew out."

The rescue chopper left Birch Mountain at six o'clock.

"They took us directly to the hospital at Fort McMurray," Fader explains, "but awhile later we were flown down to Edmonton. I don't remember any of that of course.

"I guess I talked to the emergency staff at Fort McMurray, and I told them where I lived and so on. There were some nurses there who knew me, but apparently did not recognize me because of the burns. A good friend, a lab technician, was called in from home. She did not realize it was me until someone showed her my wallet with my name in it. The doctors suggested she should leave rather than work on me, but because that would have delayed things somewhat, she stayed. I was grateful for that."

As soon as Fader was stabilized enough to travel, both he and McCormack went by medevac to the municipal airport in Edmonton, and then by land ambulance to the burn unit at the University of Alberta hospital in the city. McCormack was there for a few weeks, but half a year later was able to go back to flying. Shortly after his return, he and a passenger responded to another problem at Birch Mountain. Neither was completely at ease going there, but the trip was uneventful.

Doug Fader was in the hospital for a long time.

"I'm not sure if they really knew what to do with me at first," he said. "There were places where I was burned to the bone. My ears were gone, my hands were damaged, and even the tattoos I had on my arms were pretty well burned off. I would never recommend that kind of tattoo removal though," he jokes, "even if it is effective.

"I guess I had breathed in a lot of flame as well as

smoke, so it was awhile before I healed internally. The treatments for this were not pleasant, I guess, but luckily, I don't remember them. In fact, I have absolutely no recollection of the first eleven weeks in the hospital.

"Because I was physically scarred by the fire, the hospital had a psychiatrist come to prepare me to face the public. This woman said she would arrange a visit to a mall for me, or something like that. I told her I didn't think that would be necessary, as I had been going out in public for some time. She was surprised, I guess.

"Sure people stare at me, but that doesn't bother me at all. If I saw somebody who looked like me, I know I would stare, even if I didn't intend to. I would wonder what had happened to them, wouldn't you?

"The doctors are now going to make ears for me, and I'm really excited about that. They will drill

When asked if there were times he regretted what he had done, Doug Fader's answer is a single word: "Never!"

tungsten studs into my skull, and mould plastic ears around them. I have seen some of these, and they look great."

Doug Fader's candor in talking about his injuries is quite remarkable. So is his sense of humour, his helpfulness, and his love of life. When asked if there were times he regretted what he had done, his answer is a single word: "Never!" This from a man who has had some twenty-five operations to date, and who was unable to return to work for three years.

* * *

On December 9, 1994, Governor General Ramon Hnatyshyn bestowed the Cross of Valour on Doug Fader. And three years after the crash at Birch Mountain, Fader also received the famed Stanhope Gold Medal for the most courageous act in the British Commonwealth. It was presented by Princess Alexandra at St. James Palace in London, England.

Doug Fader happily flew to England to receive his award.

John MacLean

Tunnel of Fire

It was still dark when Christene MacLean wakened. She climbed out of bed, threw a robe around her shoulders, and went to see why she could hear corn popping at four o'clock in the morning.

But the sound was not corn popping. It was the sickening snap of shorting electrical wires. The night of March 14, 1992 would change her life forever.

* * *

Both Christene MacLean and her husband John had been born and raised on the western shore of Cape Breton Island. Apart from John's three-year stint in the army, they had always called the town of Inverness, Nova Scotia their home. In 1992 they were living in a house trailer at the top of Cabot Street, beside the high school and within sight of the ocean. They were the parents of ten children, two of whom were still at home. Derwin was twenty-two at the time, and Stephanie nineteen. Stephanie's little son, three-year-old Tyler, lived there as well.

Over the years John MacLean had a number of

jobs, from cabinetmaking to fishing. In 1992 he was doing sales work for a local firm called Cape Bald Packers. His boss there was Eric Niles.

"John MacLean was one of our best employees," Niles says. "He was hard-working, well-liked and absolutely honest. He was also a wonderful friend." Anyone in the town who knew John MacLean (and that seems to be everyone) had similar feelings.

But what happened that March night in 1992?

"Derwin and Stephanie had gone out that evening," recalls Christene. "She looked up to her big brother and he looked out for her. It was a weekend, and there was something going on in town. Johnny and I stayed home to babysit. We then could have Tyler all to ourselves.

"During the evening, though, Tyler got cranky. I don't remember now if he was getting teeth or what, but because he was upset, my husband took him in to bed with him. That worked because in no time they were both fast asleep. A bit later I went to bed in Stephanie's room. I heard her and Derwin come in later on but then I drifted off to sleep again.

"I know that it was about ten to four when I heard the popping sound out in the kitchen. I was sleeping with Stephanie, and I guess I jumped right over her and went out into the hall. Johnny and Tyler were still in bed, and Derwin was sound asleep on the sofa.

"But as soon as I came down the hall, I realized the whole place was on fire. Flames were shooting out all over. I yelled at Derwin and he went outside, then I ran and wakened Johnny and told him the trailer was on fire. He jumped right up and went out onto the deck with me. I think he was still half asleep. But then he asked me if everyone was out.

"I told him no, that Stephanie and Tyler were still in bed."

As soon as he heard this, John MacLean was suddenly wide awake. He re-entered the trailer, and despite the dense smoke and flames all around him, managed to get to Tyler's side. He took the child into his arms, and then raced back down the hall and outside. Already Tyler's clothing, face, hands and back had been burned.

"He put me down in the back of the blue Ford pickup in the driveway," Tyler explains, echoing what he has been told.

Tyler wouldn't have survived if his grandfather hadn't carried him out of the burning trailer.

"And then he went back for Stephanie," Christene adds, "because Derwin and I couldn't get to her. I had gone as far as her door, and when I touched it, it was hot. I heard the bunk beds falling in Derwin's room and I knew everything was gone. I got on my hands and knees and crawled out."

The second time he entered the house, John got no farther than the living room when the smoke

14

and flames drove him back. He retreated to the deck, gulped a mouthful of air and tried again.

That attempt was his last.

The hall was like a tunnel of fire, flames licking at the walls, even spreading across the floor. Suddenly the fibreglass material in the roof, super-heated, began to melt — just as John MacLean got to his daughter's room. The white-hot liquid gushed all over him, yet somehow he managed to get out again.

While his father had been inside, Derwin had fetched a fire extinguisher from the home of next-door neighbours Pauline and Joe Doucet. He raced there and back across frozen, lightly snow-covered ground, oblivious to the fact that he was bare-footed. Once home, he stood on the deck next to the living room and emptied the contents of the extinguisher on the engulfing flames inside. His efforts were in vain.

Christine continues the story: "Then Derwin, Johnny and I ran around to the back of the house. We thought maybe we could get Stephanie out through the bedroom window. We were all still in our night clothes of course, but that didn't matter."

As soon as the three reached the back, they screamed for Stephanie to get out. And because the window was too high to reach, John sent his son back to the deck to retrieve a stepladder stored under it. Unfortunately, the ladder was frozen solid into some ice, and could not be retrieved.

Derwin found another ladder and was able to lug it over to the back window. John MacLean held it steady as Derwin climbed up, and used his bare hands to break Stephanie's window. When he did, thick, black, acrid smoke poured from inside, choked him, and forced him back. He caught his breath, and despite the smoke, attempted to climb through the window to save his sister.

But his father interceded.

"No, son, you'll never make it," John MacLean cried as he pulled Derwin back. This act must have been heartbreaking for Mr. MacLean, for it meant that his daughter would die. But it undoubtedly prevented even more tragedy. In the end, Derwin suffered no more than shock and singed hair and eyebrows.

But John MacLean suffered much more.

John MacLean rescued his grandson, then re-entered the burning trailer to try to save his daughter.

Pauline and Joe Doucet took the MacLeans into their home. Christene carried Tyler.

"Poor Johnny, he was suffering so much," Christene explains, with tears in her eyes. "He was in terrible shape. He was burned so badly, one eye was closed, and his feet were both bleeding. When the ceiling melted, the hot plastic, or whatever it was, melted his T-shirt right into his back. Joe

Doucet called the fire department."

John O'Connor was driving the first truck to arrive on the scene. Joe Poirier was in the front seat with him, while Fire Chief Joe MacDonald rode the jump-seat just beside the driver. The firefighters did what they could, but even those wearing air packs for breathing were forced to retreat. The heat was just too intense.

In the meantime, John, Christene, Derwin and Tyler were all rushed in the same ambulance to the hospital in Inverness. Christene was uninjured, but stayed for several hours because Derwin was still in shock. The local medical staff did what they could to ease the sufferings of John MacLean and Tyler until they could be taken by ambulance to Halifax hospitals, where specialized treatment was available.

"They went alone," says Christene. "And with Derwin in the hospital, I had no way of getting to Halifax on my own. We went as soon as he was well enough though."

Neighbour Dixon Cole was there when Stephanie's body was removed from the house.

"That really hurt," he told a reporter. Stephanie had been particularly close to his wife during a family illness a few months earlier. Mr. Cole and most of the people of Inverness would take up collections, play benefit hockey games and hold church and community dinners to support the MacLean family in their hour of need.

Fortunately, Tyler was getting better. He would spend several weeks at the Izaak Walton Killam Hospital for Children in Halifax before coming home to a life without his mother.

But John MacLean was not improving. Two days after Stephanie's funeral, he died at Victoria General Hospital in Halifax. The burns he sustained to fifty percent of his body had been too much to endure. He was brought home to Christene for burial.

In the days and weeks following "the MacLean fire," as residents described it, a profound sense of loss pervaded Inverness. Anyone who had met either John or Stephanie had been touched by them, so their absence was deeply felt. When John MacLean was posthumously awarded the Cross of Valour (and the Carnegie medal for heroism) everyone felt the honour was truly deserved, even though it could never bring back the kind, courageous man who had earned it.

* * *

Christene MacLean still lives in Inverness. She is a quiet, gentle, pleasant woman who has endured much, and is now raising her grandson by herself. Tyler suffers the visible scars of the fire that killed his mother and grandfather, so Christene is reminded of that night every time she looks into his face. But the two are close, and Christene's eyes light up when Tyler is around.

For his part, Tyler remembers little of what happened. He is a cheerful, spirited boy who copes well with the scars he will always carry. In the years since the fire, he has returned to Halifax several times for treatment, and in the summer of 1997 he spent a week at a children's burn camp in Atlanta, Georgia.

In the fall of 1996 Christene suffered another fire in her home. John MacLean's Cross of Valour was almost destroyed. Luckily, it was successfully refur-

A red tricycle lies among the little that was left of the MacLeans' trailer after the fire.

bished, but his Carnegie medal had to be replaced.

Neither decoration will bring John MacLean back. But for Christene both medals are reminders of the wonderful man she married so long ago.

David Cheverie

Into an Inferno

Four months after Governor General Jeanne Sauvé presented Charlottetown police officer David Cheverie with the Star of Courage, Canada's second-highest award for bravery, this modest, soft-spoken father of two won the Cross of Valour, thus becoming the only person ever to win both awards. Doing so could easily have killed him — either time.

The first time, he entered a burning city building several times before finding and dragging a smoke victim to safety. The young constable gave the unconscious man mouth-to-mouth resuscitation as soon as they reached fresh air, and the victim recovered. Afterwards Cheverie was embarrassed when the newspapers called him a hero.

"Any of the other people I work with would have done the same thing," he said at the time, "although it feels good knowing you can actually do some good."

The next incident took place in the early hours of Saturday, May 16, 1987.

Charlottetown's Queen Street runs from the

Charlottetown Harbour, north through the downtown section of the town, past the Confederation Centre of the Arts, to Shellcourt Park, a leafy, pleasant place not far from the campus of the University of Prince Edward Island. The street is lined with modest homes, playgrounds and some small businesses.

One of the homes on Queen Street, number 446, is one that Dave Cheverie will never forget. Three children would have died there if it had not been for him.

"My partner, Clyde Sangster, and I came on duty at midnight," Cheverie recalls. "We were doing a regular patrol, south on Queen, around 2:00 A.M. Clyde was driving, and we were chatting as we went along. Up to that point, our shift had been pretty routine.

"But just as we passed some row houses near Kirkwood, I caught a glimpse of something at a window of one of them. I really didn't know what I'd seen, just that it wasn't right.

"I remember asking Clyde to stop the car, and I looked back, and then I noticed a bit of an orange glow in a living-room window. We were forty or fifty metres past the place by this time, and there was very little, if any, smoke. Just the faint glow. I got out of the car and went back."

As his partner ran across the street to the house, Sangster grabbed his radio and told the police dispatcher to call the fire department right away. Then he pulled the car well up on the west sidewalk, switched off the engine and jumped out. As he did, he noticed traces of smoke by a streetlight.

"There was no traffic at the time," Cheverie says, "and the night was clear and cool. As I ran up to the place, my worst fears were coming true; it really was a fire.

"I was familiar with these town houses, because I had been in them before, but not this one. I knew they were usually family homes, so there were likely several people inside.

"There was an aluminum screen door on the front, so I pounded on it, but there was no answer, and the thing was locked. So I broke the glass with my elbow, got the door open and realized that the wood [door] on the inside was locked as well. No one responded to my pounding this time either."

Cheverie slammed his shoulder against the wooden door. At first it didn't budge. Then he backed up and hit the door again. This time the frame along the right side cracked, and the door swung open — into an inferno.

"I remember that my first impression was of this intense heat," he says. "Everything inside was lit up.

"There was a stairway right ahead of me that led upstairs, and then to the right was a living room, or what I took to be a living room, and then a hallway that led to the back. The whole living room was on fire. You could see flames rolling up from a couch and the wall behind it.

"I dropped to the floor and tried to get in there, because my fear was that somebody was on the couch and had fallen asleep. But I couldn't make it into the room. It was just too hot and there was too much fire.

"So then I crawled on my stomach through the house to the back door, and it was locked. There was no one in the kitchen or dining room area, both of which were right behind the front room."

While there was as yet no fire in the kitchen, the smoke was thick — and deadly. Cheverie did the search on his stomach, flailing his arms and legs in all directions, because he could see nothing at all. It was only after he was satisfied no one was there that he got to his feet, held his breath, and raced down the hall and out the front door.

"By this time Clyde was just outside, talking to someone. I looked up, and there was a little boy at an upstairs window. Clyde was trying to talk him into jumping and he would catch him. The boy was crying for his mother.

"I don't think I said anything to Clyde, but I figured if the boy was calling for his mother, she must be upstairs. So I went back in and raced up the stairs. I remember the heat and the smoke and the fire, and I couldn't see my hand in front of me. So I got down on the floor and crawled to where I thought the room was, where the boy was."

In the meantime, outside on the little lawn in front of the house, Sangster pleaded with the boy to jump. The officer knew that if the child tried to come down the stairs, he might perish. Finally, standing just below the window, his arms up to make the catch, the policeman made one more appeal. At that point the boy dived head first out the window, crashed into the policeman and tumbled onto the grass. He was unhurt.

"I found the bedroom where the boy had been," Cheverie continues, "but by the time I got there, he was out. The window was open and smoke billowing out, so I stuck my head outside, got a mouthful of air, and then got down on my hands and knees to search the room.

"I could still hear the boy crying for his mother, so I figured at least one other person had to be there. And because I had been involved with fires before, I had learned how firefighters do a sweep. They go from the room they are in, right to left, and they stick to the floor, so I did that. I figured that once the firefighters got there, I could tell them certain rooms had been checked.

"But the floor in that first bedroom was so hot, I kept moving. And it seemed that every time I'd put my hand out, I would touch some clothes lying on the floor, or boxes, things like that.

"As I was finishing that room, I was going back out the way I had come in; because the door was open. By this time, I was flat on my stomach, sweeping around as far as I could reach, when I felt an arm. It was behind the door.

"I remember reaching, and pulling out something that was limp, like a rag doll. We later found out that it was a little three-year-old girl named Bryde MacLean. Anyway, I grabbed her and ran to the stairs. There was a small landing halfway down, and I remember when I got that far, the fire had spread. The flames were rolling up the wall on my right as the paint was being burned off the cement divider wall between the one townhouse and the next."

Cheverie could see the front door from the landing. He held onto the little girl, lunged down the last few steps and found himself outside. Then screams from upstairs told him the mother must be there for sure.

On the front steps now were Sangster, Constable Richard Collins, who had just arrived, and one or two others. Sangster had entered the inferno but had only reached the living room before the unbearable heat drove him back. Even then, it scorched a shoulder patch on his uniform and melted the plastic cover of his watch.

"I gave the little girl to Richard," Cheverie went on, "then I got some air and went back inside. I don't recall saying anything to anybody. I had some kind of audio exclusion, where I didn't hear if anybody spoke to me. I was too focussed on finding the mother. . . . The others couldn't figure out what was going on, because I just ran back inside.

"When I got to the top of the stairs, I heard more crying, so I got down under as much of the smoke as I could, and tried to find the second bedroom. At the time, I was wearing a leather patrol jacket, but no body armour. The heat was so intense I knew I couldn't last long in there."

Ahead of him, and to his right, was the second bedroom of the house, directly above the living-room conflagration. In this room thirteen-year-old Tara Reno and her sister, eleven-year-old Shaye, had been sleeping. Their half-brother David had woken them, screaming for his mother before diving out the window to Constable Sangster. Neither girl knew that Dave Cheverie had already rescued their little half-sister Bryde.

The girls leapt from their beds. Under Tara's bare feet the linoleum floor was bubbling in the heat, but she made it to the door and opened it. Shaye's bed was across the room where the floor was slightly cooler. She got to the open door and stumbled into the hall. Disoriented, she headed to the third bedroom instead of the stairs.

David Cheverie is the only person ever to win both the Cross of Valour and the Star of Courage.

Tara fell by her bedroom door, gulping for air, the smoke searing her throat and stinging her eyes. She cried out in fear and dragged herself up against the doorjamb, only to fall again over a vacuum cleaner. She pulled herself up a second time, almost unable to breathe. But now, David Cheverie's hand reached for her.

"I remember grabbing hold of her and putting her over my left shoulder," the police officer said. "She was in hysterics, and she more or less just fell over my shoulder. Once I got her there, I stood up for a second, and I recall trying to breathe, and getting nothing but heat in my throat. I asked the girl if anyone else was there, but she didn't seem able to answer. She just kept screaming.

"Then I started down the hall because I knew I had to get out of there. But when I came to the bathroom, I knew I should check it. It was not very big.

"There was a lot of smoke in the bathroom, but it was not as bad as in the hall, and I was able to get a breath or two and that revived me a little. No one was in there.

"Then I decided that there could only be one bedroom left and I had to check it. So I went into the hall, and then into the last room. There was a bed up by the door, and I almost fell into it.

"At this point, I was thrashing around, kicking out to see if anyone was in there, and still holding the girl on my back. Then, of course, I had no idea whether it was a girl or boy I was carrying. She was thirteen I believe, so she was fairly heavy.

"All this time, I'm thinking to myself that the mother had to be here somewhere, because the boy had been calling for her. As I continued to thrash around, I remember hitting a closet, and then all these boxes, and I thought to myself, Don't these people ever house clean? I couldn't find anyone, and there was no visibility of any sort.

"Now of course, hindsight is twenty-twenty, and I ask myself why I didn't break a window and take a breath of fresh air, but I wasn't thinking too well. I was bordering on panic: I've got to get out of here. I can't breathe. I've got to get this person out. But I've got to find the mother.

"So here I am, thrashing around, kicking every which way, and feeling all over with my free hand. Then I'd step on something, and I couldn't tell if it was a person or a toy, and I'd have to check. And then I heard a groan when I stepped on something."

Cheverie reached down and touched Shaye's unconscious little body. He went down on one knee, hooked his right arm around her waist, and lifted her under his arm. Tara reached behind him and grabbed her sister's hand. The policeman got to his feet.

At this point in his recounting of the event, Cheverie pauses, swallows hard, looks away, and then forces himself to continue. Remembering what transpired that night is obviously not easy.

"By this time, there was no air, no oxygen at all. I wasn't even holding my breath any more, I was just sucking in, sucking in fumes, but I knew I had to get out of there now. If not, the three of us were dead.

"I somehow got to the top of the stairs, and the flames were coming up them, flickering all around us. And I remember coming down through them to the landing.

"On the landing, I could see through the flames, [see] all the other police officers at the door, and behind them clear air. But now, everything was engulfed: the walls, the stairs, the floor where I stood, in a tiny space with fire under, over and on all sides.

"I looked at the front-door opening, and even though it seemed like an eternity, it was only a split second and I thought, Now what do I do? But then I know I told myself, I've got to go on; I've got to go now, because I can't breathe."

With that, carrying Tara over his shoulder and Shaye under his arm, Cheverie found deep within himself a kind of superhuman will to endure. He ran down the last few steps, raced to the open door, and dived headlong into the fresh air outside. As he hit the ground, he instinctively rolled to one side, away from the door. In that split second, he and the girls escaped one more terror.

Inside the house, the deadly concoction of gases within the smoke had built into what is called the flashover point. The front window crashed inwards, and a huge, rolling ball of fire exploded out through the front door. Cheverie lay on the lawn coughing and gasping for breath, and knew he had come very close to dying. He was not hurt, although his eyebrows, hair and moustache were singed by the flames.

"I remember lying there," he says, "and watching the fireball come out, and thanking God I knew enough to get away from in front of the open door. By that time, the firefighters were there, so they took over. One of our detectives, Mike Quinn, took the children to their grandmother. They were okay after a warm bath and a good sleep.

"Because Clyde and I had been the first officers at the scene, it was our responsibility to investigate what transpired. I remember talking to the firefighters and telling them which rooms I had checked. It was still my belief that the mother was either in that third bedroom, or she was dead on the living-room couch. I was so convinced that I asked the station to have the coroner on standby.

"Then I remember going back in after the fire had been beaten down, and looking around, poking through soot and debris with the firefighters. But there was nothing there and I was so relieved. It turned out that the mother had not been in the house at all. She returned home some time later.

The cause of the fire, we determined eventually, was arson."

* * *

In the years since the house at 446 Queen Street burned, Dave Cheverie has kept in touch with David, the boy who jumped from the upper window, and the three girls he saved.

Tara, in particular, has had a unique career. She is an accomplished singer who enjoys international acclaim. On her first compact disc, under her professional name, Tara MacLean, her beautiful, haunting voice carries no hint of the trauma of that terrible night in 1987. In the liner notes to the CD however, she gives thanks where thanks are due: to "David Cheverie, for your courage."

René Jalbert

"Stop Firing!"

Just before 9:45 on the morning of May 8, 1984, a man dressed in military camouflage drove a beige Buick Skyhawk up to the south doors of the National Assembly building in Quebec City. He switched off the ignition, carefully adjusted the beret he was wearing and reached across the seat for two 9mm sub-machine guns. He then stepped from the car, slung one weapon over his shoulder, cradled the other in his hands and walked to the side door.

At about the same time, journalists at radio station CJRP, some two kilometres away, were listening to a tape brought to them a few minutes earlier. The red-bearded man who delivered the recording had worn military fatigues and had a hunting knife dangling from his thigh. He told the woman who received the cassette not to play it until after ten A.M. She passed the message to her boss, broadcaster André Arthur.

Even though Arthur was on the air at the time, he told his staff to listen to the tape right away. The appearance of the man who had delivered it had been alarming.

The first five or six minutes on the cassette were a rambling commentary, in French, about the Parti Québécois and the failings of its language policies. But then the male voice turned more strident: "The government which presently is in office is going to be destroyed. . . . I believe these are people who have done a lot of wrong, not only to the French language in Quebec, but in Canada. What I am doing isn't for me, but for people in the future who speak the French language. . . . There is no longer anyone who can stop me. . . . I want to destroy the Parti Québécois."

The staff at CJRP had heard enough. André Arthur phoned the police. Unfortunately, the call came too late.

The man with the machine guns bounded up the five steps to the legislature doors. He pulled the right one open and stepped inside.

The receptionist on duty at the time was an outgoing young woman named Jacynthe Richard. She looked up as the man entered, smiled and started to say good morning to him. Her greeting became a scream as the man swung the muzzle of one of the machine guns toward her, steadied himself for a fraction of a second and squeezed the trigger.

A volley of shots echoed across the hall and reverberated down the marble corridors of the government building. Several bullets tore into Richard's right arm and chest and knocked her backward toward the door of an adjoining office. As she fell, the gunman pointed his firearm at a red emergency telephone nearby. He fired a single burst from the weapon and the telephone disintegrated. He then turned away from the critically wounded woman and began walking to the right, down a corridor that runs parallel to Grande Allée, Quebec City's best-known street.

As he went, the gunman continued to shoot — at the floor, the walls, the ceiling and anyone who moved. The wreckage he left behind evidenced a man out of control. When he came to the end of the first corridor, the gunman turned left and moved toward the main doors of the parliament. Coming toward him was security guard Denis Samson, who had been in the front lobby when the firing started. Samson was on his way to see what was happening.

He did not get far.

The gunman shot the guard in the abdomen and Samson crumpled. Then the intruder headed for the staircase leading to the Blue Room, the ornate Legislative Chamber that is the Quebec National Assembly. It was here that he expected to find the objects of his quest.

While the vicious onslaught was underway in the parliament buildings, a sixty-three-year-old ex-soldier named René Jalbert was driving the two kilometres from his home to his office in the National Assembly building. Major Jalbert had been a member of the famed French Canadian Royal 22nd Regiment, often called the Van Doos, and was a veteran of the Second World War and Korea. On May 8, 1984, he was the sergeant-at-arms at the National Assembly, and in that role was responsible for its security.

Jalbert had the radio on in his car, but his mind was not on the music. That morning at 10:00 a parliamentary committee was meeting in the Blue

Room, and before the meeting began Jalbert wanted to be sure everything was ready.

Directly across Grande Allée from the National Assembly is a large cement-and-glass office building locally known as H Block, or "The Bunker," where government officials have their offices. Under the building is a reserved parking area. On that cold, rainy Tuesday morning Jalbert was happy to be able to leave his car indoors.

The sergeant-at-arms parked, locked his car and walked through a tunnel under Grande Allée

The Quebec National Assembly, where Lortie decided to take his revenge.

toward his office on the basement level of the National Assembly building. Just as he emerged from the tunnel he was told that someone was shooting upstairs.

By this time the gunman was two floors above, in the Legislative Chamber itself. He had rushed past the wounded security guard and up the stairs toward the mezzanine level of the building, where the parliamentary restaurant is situated. Fortunately he did not realize that several members of the National Assembly — his intended targets — were in the restaurant at the time. He was too busy firing his machine gun at the carpet, at the stairs, at the walls and at fifty-four-year-old Camille Lepage, a parliamentary messenger who happened to be descending the stairs at the time. Lepage died quickly.

Inside the restaurant, then Finance Minister Jacques Parizeau and others were having breakfast. When the sound of gunfire was heard in the lobby below, someone quickly closed the restaurant doors, but bullets crashed through them. One nicked the desk where the cash register sat, but no one in the room was injured. The gunman continued up the stairs. "I have a gang to kill on the third floor," he shouted.

There is a large, carpeted landing on the top floor of the building. On the right was the Red Room, where groups of schoolchildren had paused in their tour of the parliament buildings. When they heard the gunfire on the stairs, guides and teachers closed the doors and ordered the children to lie on the floor. Their quick thinking worked: all the students were later evacuated safely.

The gunman turned left and threw open the doors of the Blue Room. Now at last he would come face to face with the members of the National Assembly, the majority of them men and women of the Parti Québécois, whom he believed were doing wrong to the French-speaking populace of Quebec and of Canada as a whole. Now he would somehow right those wrongs.

But the chamber was almost empty.

"Where are the legislators? I am going to kill them!" the gunman screamed in French. "Where have they all gone? I am going to bring down this government. I am going to rid the province of this government."

The man looked around the room, an expression of disappointment on his face. "I don't see them," he wailed. Then he began blasting away with a machine gun — "left and right, up and down, everywhere," according to a man who was there at the time. A few civil servants and others were present, preparing the room for the coming meeting. One of them was Georges Boyer, fifty-nine, a former military policeman in the Canadian Forces, and since 1980 an Assembly employee. He was shot in the legs but managed to crawl behind a press table at the rear of the room. He lay there for over an hour and lost so much blood that he died later that day.

Another visitor was Roger Lefrançois, who worked for Quebec's office of the director of elections. He and a colleague had just entered the Blue Room as the gunman arrived. Lefrançois looked around to see what was happening and was splattered by a volley of shells from point-blank range. His body jerked backwards, his glasses flew off and blood poured from his mouth. He died where he fell.

Rejean Dionne was a cameraman in the National Assembly. He heard the gunman enter the Chamber, but quickly dropped to the floor and lay motionless between two desks. He felt no pain at first, but Dionne later realized he had been shot in the right elbow.

The desperate gunman stormed the length of the room and shot at everything in sight, including four of the five wall-mounted television cameras used to film debates in the Chamber. He walked past the desk used by then Premier René Levesque, past the Speaker's chair at the front of the room, and out into a small lobby adjacent to the Chamber. The lobby opens in turn into a hallway where there is an elevator leading to the lower floors.

He walked to the elevator, sprayed the control buttons and the stainless steel door with bursts from one of his guns and shot several rounds down the hall. Then he turned and headed back to the Blue Room.

By the time the terrified occupants of the smoke-filled lobby dared look up, the gunman had returned to the Blue Room, walked up the three steps to the Speaker's platform and ensconced himself in the Speaker's chair. As he settled back and surveyed the historic Chamber in front of him, he brought one of the machine guns up to chest level and began firing everywhere.

"I heard a burst of fire from an automatic weapon as I stepped off the elevator," recalls René Jalbert, who had arrived to investigate the shooting. "There were a lot of 9mm shells lying around in the small lobby just behind the Chamber, so I knew it had to be a machine gun of some kind. I decided to be careful and to go very slowly."

Jalbert picked his way through the shells and the debris that had fallen from the walls and ceiling, and cautiously made his way to the Blue Room. He entered the Chamber through the same door the gunman had used a moment or so earlier.

"When I looked around from behind the Speaker's chair, I could see the length of the room," says Jalbert, "and I could see where the fellow was firing. Mr. Levesque's desk was to my right, and a television camera was above it and slightly to the rear. The guy was spraying that side of the room with bullets, and I could see both the wood on Mr. Levesque's desk and the plaster on the right wall exploding. If the Premier or any of the other députés had been there, they would have died for sure. I also noticed a strong smell of gunpowder in the air."

Finally there was silence and Jalbert made his move. "Stop firing," he yelled in French. "I want to talk to you!"

The gunman gaped at Jalbert; then he said "Yes" and stopped shooting.

Because the gunman had responded to his first request, Jalbert decided to carry on with the same approach. "What are you doing here?" he asked as he stood beside a little table next to the Speaker's chair. "Don't you see that this room has been recently renovated? You're wrecking everything. Why are you doing this? You're a taxpayer and I'm a taxpayer. This is costing us money."

The gunman gaped at Jalbert. The sergeant-at-arms continued. "I see you are a soldier. I'm a soldier too — at least I'm a veteran. If you promise not to shoot, I'll take my wallet out and I'll show you my discharge card."

The man in the Speaker's chair was obviously nervous. His face was pale and he was sweating heavily. At times he seemed to have trouble getting his breath. He waved his gun around, pointing at Jalbert.

"I didn't want him to think I was pulling a gun," explains Jalbert, in recalling the incident. "I did everything slowly because I didn't want him to explode." Cautiously Jalbert reached into his pocket, withdrew his wallet, took out the card and handed it to the gunman. The man studied it for awhile, then handed it back.

"Look," Jalbert said to the gunman, "I told you I was a soldier and I proved it to you. I showed you my card. Now I see that you are a soldier, or at least you are dressed like a soldier, but I'm not sure if you really are one. Have you some identification?"

"Yes," answered the gunman and he handed Jalbert a card from his pocket. The inscription read: LORTIE, DENIS—CORPORAL. The date of birth indicated that the man was twenty-five.

"From then on, I called him either 'Denis' or 'Corporal,' " says Jalbert. "And I kept on talking and asking him questions because I wanted to calm him down and get his mind off that machine gun. I didn't want to get shot."

"Denis," said Jalbert to the gunman, "do you smoke? I would like a cigarette and I'll give you one."

Lortie said he did not smoke.

"Then I want a smoke," said Jalbert. "Do you mind if I smoke?"

Lortie replied that he did not mind, so Jalbert lit the first of almost two packs of cigarettes he would smoke in the next four hours.

"Well, if you don't smoke," the sergeant-at-arms asked the gunman, "what do you do? Do you take drugs or something?"

"My drug is gum," answered Lortie.

"What kind of gum?" Jalbert asked.

"Dentyne. It helps increase the saliva in my mouth," Lortie explained.

René Jalbert's quick thinking calmed down the desperate gunman.

Corporal Lortie was chewing gum at the time, so Jalbert suggested he chew another piece — anything to calm the young man down. But instead of doing as Jalbert wanted, Lortie reached into his mouth, took out his false teeth and threw them on the floor. Then he took off his beret and flung it over a microphone in front of the Speaker's chair. Jalbert did not react. Instead, he asked the gunman why he was doing all the shooting.

"I knew he had some kind of problem," Jalbert recalls, "and I told him we should get out of the Chamber so we could talk. I told him I was there to help him. What I did not say was that I was afraid some of the people who were supposed to be coming to the ten o'clock meeting would show up and he would kill them. At this stage, I did not know that he had murdered three people and injured thirteen others. I didn't even know some were in the Chamber. I saw no one when I entered."

The others in the room were hiding behind desks and remaining perfectly still. Later one of them recalled what the ordeal was like for her: "At first I thought I was the only one alive," she said. "I couldn't hear a thing. Then I heard Mr. Jalbert and I said to myself: 'Thank you, God.'"

At least one other person knew what was happening in the Blue Room. Johanne Tanguay was in another area of the building, but it was she who operated the only television camera that had not been wrecked by gunfire. The camera was run by remote control, and it gave Tanguay a view from the gallery above the floor of the house. The entire interchange between Lortie and Jalbert in the Legislature was videotaped. "From time to time,

Lortie took shots at my camera," she recalls, "so I stopped moving it to record what was happening."

Tanguay also noticed a movement that Jalbert later explained: "Out of the corner of my eye," he said, "I saw a flash of blond hair behind one of the desks. It was one of the pages. I motioned her to stay down and then I started to negotiate for the release of everyone in the room, but I still didn't know who was there. I asked Lortie."

Lortie pointed to different areas of the room. "There are some there, and there, and there," he said.

"Look," Jalbert said to the gunman, "I want to help you. But we should be discussing your problem alone. If there are people here, you have to promise to let them go out safely. Then, when we are alone, we can talk."

After much hesitation Lortie consented, and those who were hiding in the chamber walked out, some of them bleeding. Once they were apparently alone, Jalbert and Lortie continued to talk for almost forty minutes. At one stage Jalbert noticed a security guard in the gallery at the opposite end of the chamber. He called to the guard and ordered two cups of coffee. When the coffee arrived Jalbert gave a cup to the killer and drank the other himself. Gradually the gunman was becoming calmer.

"As we were having coffee, I asked Lortie if he realized there might be policemen in the gallery who would shoot him," Jalbert recalls.

"Oh, that's all right. I couldn't care less," Lortie answered.

Jalbert later admitted that the reply chilled him. "I knew then that he was prepared to die, that he expected to die, but I had no intention of dying with him, so I knew we had to get out of there. I tried again to talk him into going to my office."

This time, Jalbert got his wish.

Lortie got up, picked up his guns and followed the sergeant-at-arms from the room. And even though the man behind him was a killer and held a gun to his back, Jalbert never flinched. He led Denis Lortie to the elevator, and after some difficulty getting it to work because it had been shot up earlier, managed to open the door and ride it to the basement.

When the two men arrived at Jalbert's office his secretary, Lucienne Lebel, was on the phone. The police had called her earlier and asked her to remain in her office and to lock the door. When she heard it being unlocked, she relaxed. Only the cleaning staff and her boss had office keys.

"Corporal Lortie, I would like you to meet my secretary, Madame Lebel," said Jalbert, in an attempt to let the killer know that all was well. "Madame Lebel, Corporal Lortie."

Lortie shook Lebel's hand and kissed her on the cheek. She smiled at him, thankful that the long, violent nightmare was finally over. Her boss was safe at last, and this polite young man with him must be a member of the police SWAT team, which she knew was somewhere in the building.

She turned and accidentally knocked over a small flower vase on her desk. When she reached for some tissues to sponge up the water, Lortie smiled and assisted her. Then Jalbert invited the corporal to sit down.

"May I talk to my secretary, Denis?" Jalbert asked.

"Yes, of course," Lortie responded.

"Madame Lebel," said Jalbert, "go up to the

restaurant and get a cup of coffee."

"But Mr. Jalbert, the restaurant will be closed now," she answered, "and I really don't need a cup of coffee."

"Madame Lebel!" snapped the sergeant-at-arms with feigned harshness. "Go and get a cup of coffee! I want to talk to Corporal Lortie alone."

The bewildered Lebel frowned at her boss and left the office. As soon as she was outside the door, SWAT team members told her who Lortie was and whisked her away. She was aghast at what had just happened.

Jalbert had decided at this point that if Lortie became violent again only two people would die: Jalbert himself, murdered by the corporal, and Lortie, by suicide. "Because we were alone, and Lortie had no one to perform for, I felt I might convince him to surrender," Jalbert explained.

"Denis," he said, "you have two hands and two weapons. Why don't you pull another chair up beside you and you can put one of your machine guns on it. Then you can put the other one on the desk in front of you and it will be handy if you need it. That way you will have both hands free and we can talk."

Lortie did as Jalbert suggested.

Major Jalbert then began a wide-ranging, four-hour discussion with the murderer. Some of the topics they covered were army life, politics, travel and sports. Lortie's reasons for his actions were jumbled, just as they had been on tape. But Jalbert was gaining his trust, and the corporal began to relax.

Then the phone rang.

Lortie jumped, put his hand on a gun and glared at Jalbert.

"May I answer the phone?" the major asked.

"Yes," the corporal agreed.

The caller was Jalbert's wife Nanette. She was phoning from work because she had heard rumours of trouble at the National Assembly. At this point she had no idea that her husband was in any way involved, much less that he was staring down the barrel of a 9mm sub-machine gun.

"Are you all right, René? What's going on?"

"Nothing is going on now, dear," answered her husband. "There was a bit of trouble awhile ago, but I'm a little busy right now. I can't talk to you. I'll call you back."

"Okay," answered Nanette Jalbert. She hung up.

The gunman relaxed again and the conversation between the killer and the sergeant-at-arms continued.

Then the telephone jangled a second time.

Lortie flinched and pulled a loaded pistol from his belt. He pulled the hammer back, set the weapon on the desk in front of him and watched to see what Jalbert would do.

"May I answer the phone, Denis?" the major asked.

"Yes," answered Corporal Lortie.

The second caller was a journalist. Jalbert talked for a moment and hung up. After that several reporters called, and each time the telephone rang Lortie became more and more upset.

"The calls from the journalists were really bothering me," admits Jalbert. "There were so many that I had to start hanging up on them just to stop the ringing. I could see that Lortie was getting worked up, and the phone was making what I was trying to do more difficult. I would get him calmed down, the phone would ring and I would have to start all over again. Finally I convinced him that what he had in mind was impossible, that he should surrender."

"There's no way!" Lortie retorted vehemently. "I won't surrender to the Quebec police. I want to be treated humanely."

Jalbert was not sure what this comment meant. But when he heard it he decided to try another approach.

"Look, you're a soldier, I'm a soldier. If you agree, I will arrange for you to surrender to the military police. I know they will treat you fairly." Lortie was unmoved, and Jalbert recalls that he must have made the suggestion at least twenty times. He also pointed out to the killer that he could not stay where he was forever. Finally the words that Jalbert longed to hear were spoken.

"Okay, I'll surrender."

Jalbert immediately telephoned his friend Colonel Armand Roy at nearby Canadian Forces Base Valcartier. The sergeant-at-arms began to explain his predicament when Roy interrupted.

"Yes, René, I know. I'm listening to the radio here. Can I help you?"

Jalbert asked Roy to send two military police officers to the Assembly building because Corporal Lortie had agreed to surrender to them. Roy said they would be there in half an hour.

"Corporal," Jalbert said, "do you want to talk to Colonel Roy? Then you will know I've been telling you the truth. He is going to send the military police."

Lortie nodded, picked up his pistol in one hand and the phone in the other and talked to Armand Roy. The conversation lasted about two minutes. Then the killer sat down, placed the revolver on the desk in front of him and looked at Jalbert.

"Denis," said Jalbert, "it's almost noon and I'm hungry. Are you hungry?"

"No," responded Lortie.

"Well, even if you're not," Jalbert went on, "I am. I'm going to order some sandwiches and coffee for us."

Lortie didn't say anything.

Jalbert picked up the telephone and called the Office of Security for the building. A SWAT team member answered and the sergeant-at-arms ordered sandwiches for two. Fifteen minutes later the food was delivered in a paper bag and placed on the floor in the corridor, about eight metres from Jalbert's office.

Major Jalbert opened the door to the hall, walked slowly to the sandwiches and picked up the bag. All the way, Lortie had one of his machine guns trained on Jalbert's back.

"As I was going for the sandwiches, I didn't know whether he would shoot me in the back or not." Jalbert winces as he recalls the incident. "I saw two SWAT guys in the corridor, but I knew I would be dead before they could take Lortie. At that time, I was afraid."

Jalbert returned and Lortie locked the door. After they had eaten, the sergeant-at-arms asked Lortie why he had done what he had done, why he had done such a stupid thing. The young soldier started to cry.

"He cried for two or three minutes," said Jalbert, "and then he felt better. I knew then that he was back to normal. All morning I had been trying to establish a relationship of confidence between us, and I now knew I was getting somewhere. I pointed out to him that he had agreed to surrender to the military police, and that it was time we set forth the type of protocol that would be expected."

Jalbert then talked to Lortie as a soldier. "You are a corporal. I am a major. From now on, you will address me as Major and I will address you as Corporal. Is that understood?"

"Yes, Major!" Lortie barked.

"Well then," Jalbert said, "we will now arrange for your surrender."

Half an hour later Corporal Denis Lortie was in custody.

* * *

Denis Lortie was convicted on three charges of first-degree murder on February 13, 1985. The seven women and five men of the jury nodded assent when Quebec Superior Court Judge Ivan Mignault sentenced the young father of two to life imprisonment, without parole for twenty-five years.

At 11:00 A.M. on Friday, November 9, 1984 in Ottawa, Governor General Jeanne Sauvé conferred the Cross of Valour on Major René M. Jalbert. Then the sergeant-at-arms flew back to Quebec to continue overseeing security at the National Assembly.

Bob Teather

Trapped Undersea!

When the phone wakened him at four that morning, the policeman knew the call would be an emergency. He switched on his bedside light and answered the first ring. The voice on the line was familiar.

"Bob, listen closely," said the caller. "Rescue Coordination in Vancouver have just told me they have an overturned fishing boat with two men trapped inside it. They need a couple of divers right away. I'll pick you up in ten minutes."

The caller hung up.

Royal Canadian Mounted Police Corporal Robert Teather bounded out of bed, pulled a sweatsuit over his pajamas and told his wife Susan about the call.

"Not again!" she remarked. "Bob, be careful."

"Sure."

He kissed her on the cheek and dashed out of the room. Five minutes later Corporal Tim Kain, RCMP Dive Team supervisor, pulled the police van into the driveway.

Teather tossed his diving gear in the rear door and ran around to the passenger side. He had hardly got into his seat when Kain tramped the accelerator and the vehicle shot into the darkened streets of Delta, British Columbia. "We have to meet a Hovercraft at the government dock at Steveston," said Kain as he switched on the emergency lights and siren. "The sooner we get there, the better. Apparently the guys in the boat won't last long."

Teather says the drive from his home to the fishing village of Steveston was hair-raising. "It was a Code 3 — red lights and sirens all the way. Part of the trip was on a freeway, and when we swung off it we had a police escort the rest of the way. All the stop streets were cleared for us and we really flew. There isn't much traffic at 4:00 A.M., and we did the run in eighteen minutes. In traffic it takes an hour."

As the divers were racing toward their destination, the two trapped fishermen managed to remain reasonably calm. They were boxed inside the inverted engine room of the little troller *Respond*, a fifteen-metre fishing boat that had capsized when it collided with the *Rimba Meranti*, a Malaysian lumber carrier on its way to Vancouver.

The accident happened shortly after 3:00 A.M. on September 26, 1981 in the Strait of Georgia, some two kilometres out from the mouth of the Fraser River. A lookout on the freighter had failed to see the tiny white boat until it was too late to change course. The huge bulbous bow of the Malaysian ship had gone under the fishing vessel and tossed it aside like a cork.

Initially the captain of the *Respond*, twenty-four-year-old Rod Larden, thought his boat had hit a submerged log. But then, as the little boat began to list farther and farther and failed to right herself, he realized what had happened. By the time the *Respond* was on its side, Larden and twenty-three-year-old Frank Michelanko, the second man on board, along with Larden's black Labrador, Tiki, were all bracing themselves for what was coming.

Within seconds the *Respond* was upside down, with the two men and the dog lying on the ceiling of the wheelhouse. Torrents of water began rushing in. Tiki began to whine, and in her terror looked for safety.

Larden glanced above him in the direction of the surface. The only thing farther up was the engine room. He scrambled into it, heaving Tiki up with him. The dog was shaking with fear.

Frank was not a swimmer, and the swiftly rising water drove him to the edge of panic. He had picked himself up as soon as the boat became stable, but then had watched in horror as the water rose — first to his knees, then to his waist and shoulders.

Rod yelled from above, urging Frank to climb, and extended a hand to bring his friend to safety. The task was not easy. Frank weighed over ninety kilograms, while Rod was about thirty kilograms lighter. Nevertheless Frank succeeded in getting up to the engine room seconds before the wheelhouse became totally submerged. As it did, Rod grabbed an emergency flashlight.

It was not until both men were actually in the engine room that they realized the motor was still running. When Rod reached to shut it off, hot oil gushed over his neck and shoulders. He pulled back with a start.

Then the lights went out.

The sudden darkness was as unexpected as it

was eerie. For a moment neither man spoke, and although she whimpered once or twice, even Tiki became still. The claustrophobic silence was overwhelming.

The men were trapped.

On the surface, the *Rimba Meranti* immediately radioed the Canadian Coast Guard and told them of the collision. The Coast Guard broadcast a distress call. Two ships close by sped to the scene.

The night was pitch dark — there was no moonlight — and the floating hull of the upturned fishing

Bob Teather looking up from the engine room where Respond's *crew, and Tiki, were trapped.*

vessel was no more than a dark object on a black sea. The lights and the motor had died, and there had been no Mayday broadcast. Calls by loud-hailer and radio went unanswered, and the four men on the *Tsonoqua*, the first vessel to reach the scene, surmised that the occupants of the boat were dead.

They decided to pull their boat up beside the *Respond*. As they did, they kept yelling. Down inside the hull of the upturned ship the men and the dog in the oily hell heard a sound. Rod switched on his flashlight. Tiki sat up, stopped shivering and yelped.

Silence.

Then the sound outside came again. Frank and Rod looked at each other, and their beaming faces said there might be hope. Rod grabbed a wrench, pounded on the aluminum hull and listened.

"Is there anybody there?" came a muffled voice from outside. "Is there anybody there?"

Rod pounded again and Tiki barked. "Yes, two of us," he shouted, "and my dog."

"Good. We'll try to help you," said the voice. The *Tsonoqua* stood by, and a coast guard Hovercraft arrived. As soon as the skipper of the Hovercraft learned that men were alive inside the fishing boat, he radioed for divers, spun his craft around and sped toward Steveston for Tim Kain and Bob Teather. But as his machine raced over the fifteen kilometres to get them, he found himself wondering if they would ever be able to save the men in that sunken hull. He knew the pocket of air under the *Respond* would not be there for long.

"There were four crewmen on the Hovercraft when it met us," recalls Bob Teather today. "The captain, a navigator and two others. As well, a couple of policemen left their cruiser and helped us load the diving gear, oxygen resuscitators and so on. This job generally takes at least twenty minutes. That night it was completed in five.

"The trip out to the boat took about fifteen minutes because the Hovercraft they were using cruises at close to eighty kilometres an hour. The sea was rolling slightly, and I don't recall any stars. You could see a few lights from Vancouver, away off in the distance. Tim and I started to put on our diving suits as we went along."

Meanwhile a second boat, a tug, had arrived at the scene and switched a couple of spotlights on the *Respond*. For a time the situation seemed more hopeful. But then it became clear that finding an escape route for the men down below would be difficult. Larden had attempted to hold his breath and dive down under his floating prison, but he was unable to open a jammed door that blocked the passageway leading outside. He had been driven back to the engine room as the *Respond* settled lower and lower. By the time the coast guard Hovercraft arrived, the trapped men's air pocket was no bigger than the interior of a compact car.

"The Hovercraft skipper slowed down as we came up to the scene," says Teather, "because we didn't want to jostle the fishing boat too much. When we were settled in the water and the big searchlights from the Hovercraft were switched on, the place was quite bright.

"Tim and I were in our diving suits by this time, but we didn't have our diving tanks on yet. When the forward hatch of the Hovercraft was lowered, we walked down the gangplank to the edge of the water. That was when the enormity of the whole thing hit me.

"We looked over at the upturned hull and I thought of the poor guys down inside it. I knew right then that whoever went down for them would likely never come out alive. It really terrified me. After we both looked on in silence for a second or two, Tim put his hand on my shoulder and said, 'My God, this is not a drill.' I felt sick."

As soon as he was close enough to the *Respond* to touch it, Teather took his diver's knife and scratched a long mark on the ship's hull, just at the water line. "I knew it was going to be a few minutes before we went in, and I wanted to see what the boat was doing. Ten minutes later, when my mark was fifteen centimetres lower in the water, I knew time was running out. The boat was sinking. On top of that, the wind was picking up and the sea was becoming choppy.

"I needed to know as much about the situation as I could, so I climbed up on the hull and asked the guys inside three questions: 'Do you speak English?' 'How many are there?' and 'Is anybody hurt?' I wanted to know if I could talk to them, and if I did get inside, I wanted some idea of what I could expect. Their answers were muffled, but by putting your ear close to the hull, you could hear pretty well.

"Then Tim and I put on our tanks, masks and fins and swam down under the *Respond* to see what things were like. The whole place was a real mess. There were fishing lines hanging down all over the place and more or less drifting with the current.

There was also a lot of debris and patches of oily scum, and that made it hard to see very far.

"We had hand lanterns, and with the light we managed to locate a Dutch door leading to the passageway down the centre of the boat. The door itself was in two sections, so that ordinarily the top could be opened, or both parts could be. Anyway, one half wouldn't budge, so we knew if we were able to get the guys out it would be a tight squeeze. That was when we realized only one of us could do the dive. There would not be room for both."

The two divers surfaced. The first thing they noticed was that the sea was rougher now and the wind stronger than it had been. An earlier suggestion that a hole be cut into the hull of the *Respond* so the fishermen could escape was tossed aside as impractical. The boat would go down like a rock if the air pocket was disturbed. But now almost everyone on the scene knew that, air pocket or not,

"I knew right then that whoever went down for [the men] would likely never come out alive."

rough water might soon sink the ailing craft.

"When Tim and I realized how bad things actually were, we looked at each other and decided I would be the one to go down. Tim would stay in the water and take the men from me if I could get them out. At this stage, I really did not want to do the dive. I honestly felt I'd never come out. However, I also believe that when you decide to be a cop you are expected to put your life on the line if necessary. That comes with the territory."

The divers worked feverishly on last-minute preparations for what lay ahead. The pressure regulator at the top of Tim Kain's diving tank was cannibalized and Teather's tank was rigged in such a way that it would have an extra breathing apparatus. Then Teather slid into the water and the rescue attempt began. It was 5:40 A.M.

"I spent a short time tying the fishing lines out of the way," he recalls. "I knew that if I did get one or both of the men we could drown just by getting tangled up on our way out.

"Once I had the lines tied, I tried to open the other half of the Dutch door, but still got nowhere. Finally, I swam in through the open half and immediately got lost. I had a light with me, but there was almost no visibility. There was a lot of oil and gasoline in the water, but as well, the whole passageway was obscured by hundreds of bits of soggy dog kibble.

"There was a small anteroom just inside the Dutch door, and that was where I got lost. I did a couple of turnarounds somehow, but finally got back to the door and started over. This time I swam along the floor, which was my ceiling. There were cupboard doors open and junk all over the place, so

57

I tried to clear a passage as I went. Then I felt something hit my head."

By this time Larden, Michelanko and Tiki were confined in the tiniest of spaces. Larden shone his flashlight into the murky water as a guide for Teather. The policeman was facing away from the light and didn't see it, so Larden had to hit him on the head with a broomstick to get his attention.

Moments later, the trapped fishermen saw the man who represented their only hope of getting out alive.

"Hi there," said Teather when he came face to face with the two. "How are you?"

"My first thought was that these guys were really cool after what they'd been through," he recalls. "We had a brief, two-second conversation and then I asked who was going first."

"He is," Rod Larden answered. "I'm the skipper. Frank goes first."

Teather said, "Okay, Frank, get in the water and I'll teach you how to dive."

Michelanko apparently thought the mountie was standing on something.

"He moved over beside me," explains Teather, "and the next thing I knew we were both under the water. I didn't know he couldn't swim, and I guess he grabbed me to steady himself. We both went under and I swallowed some oil. There was a five-centimetre film of oil, gasoline and kibble on the top of the water, so everything you touched was slimy. When I finally got Frank back up where I wanted him, I threw up."

Teather wiped the oil from the oxygen mouthpiece and showed Frank what to do next.

"I breathed through one and he used the other. Then I told him to hold the mouthpiece in with his right hand, and to place his left on my tank belt, at the nape of my neck."

Michelanko did as he was told.

"Now, Frank," Teather continued, "hold on tight and I'll take you out on my back."

The big man nodded.

The two ducked under the water and started down toward the engine room hatch that opened in the floor of the central passageway. They managed to squeeze through the hatch, but then the confined space, the darkness and the fact that he could not swim got to Michelanko. He panicked.

He began to flail around, out of control. He wrapped his legs around Teather's waist and grabbed the slim policeman around the neck. Teather lost his mask and his oxygen mouthpiece. The two tumbled over and over in the tiny underwater chamber, and Teather's lungs ached for air. He choked on the oily water and kibble and began retching as he desperately attempted to get his bearings and find his mouthpiece. Each time he threw up, the involuntary contraction of his throat caused him to suck in more of the putrid water around him.

Finally, luckily, he was able to locate the missing oxygen line.

"I jammed it back into my mouth," he recalls with a shudder, "but I was still without my mask and I had to let go of the light I carried because I needed both hands just to get the mouthpiece back in and try to steady myself. Frank was still clutched to me, so I opened my eyes to see if I could tell where we were.

"All I could see was a faint greenish glow, which I knew must be coming from the floodlights outside. I went into a fetal position and Frank's grip was not so tight. Somehow we got to the Dutch door, but I really don't know how we ever got through it. I do know the squeeze was really tight and Frank must have felt like a barnacle being scraped off the bottom of a boat. Anyway, he held on and I remember bracing my feet against the door sill and pushing myself toward the surface.

"Because I couldn't see very well I came up on the far side of the boat, away from the Hovercraft. When we got to the surface, I went into the fetal position again in order to ease Frank's hold on me. Then I screamed for help, and in ten seconds Tim Kain was beside me, prying Frank off my back. The gasoline had burned Frank's eyes and he couldn't see, and I don't think he knew where we were. He and Tim struggled a bit, but Tim was able to get him to the Hovercraft."

Teather rested in the water for a few seconds before getting ready to go down for Larden.

"I had trouble getting everything together," he says, "because whatever I touched had a film of oil over it. My mask had been looped around my neck, under the oxygen line, so it had to be wiped off. As I was doing this, Tim swam back to me and asked how I was. He said he would go for the second man, but I told him there wasn't time."

With that, Teather popped his mouthpiece back in and dived for the Dutch door. A minute later he was in the engine room talking to Rod Larden.

"Okay, Rod, you're next."

"What about Tiki?" asked Larden. "Take Tiki first, I'll wait."

"No, I want to take you now, Rod. I'll come back for Tiki," Teather responded.

The second fisherman grasped Teather and the two drifted down, out of the engine room. This time the rescue went as planned. Teather was able to maintain his direction, and Larden floated out with relative ease. Tim Kain met them on the surface and hoisted Larden from the water.

When he saw that the second man was safe, Teather told Kain that Tiki was next.

"Oh no, she isn't," Kain retorted. "You've done enough." He grabbed Teather's harness and hauled his friend to safety.

Up on the Hovercraft the crew was cheering.

* * *

Several hours after the accident the *Respond* was towed to shore and another diver went to the engine room for Tiki. He brought her out alive.

On Friday, June 24, 1983, Bob Teather received the Cross of Valour and Tim Kain the Medal of Bravery for their heroic action in the rescue of Rod Larden and Frank Michelanko.

Anna Lang

"Lana, I'll be back!"

Anna Lang of Nauwigewauk, New Brunswick, looks back at the events that led up to her winning of the Cross of Valour as if they were all part of a terrible dream, a nightmare that somehow came true, a hell so horrible she is amazed she escaped it.

At noon on Tuesday, September 9, 1980, forty-two-year-old Lang and her friend, thirty-one-year-old Lana Walsh, were returning from Saint John where they had been working out in a city gym. With them, in the rear seat of Anna's new red two-door Buick, was Walsh's four-year-old son Jaye. Anna was driving.

Because the day was warm, Lana had opened the passenger-side window. The two women chatted about the events of the morning, and about the dangerous situation some ten kilometres ahead, at the Hammond River bridge.

The bridge is a hundred-metre long, two-lane reinforced concrete structure carrying provincial Highway 1 over the Hammond River, thirty kilometres northeast of Saint John. The traffic deck of the bridge is nine metres above the water, and is supported by five massive, tapered pillars. At the overpass the river is about eighty metres wide and over two metres deep. The current is not strong.

Drivers approaching the bridge from either direction must first negotiate a series of hazardous downhill curves. But on this day the major hazard at the Hammond River was the bridge itself. For over a week the south lane had been closed.

"They were replacing the right guardrail of the thing," recalls Anna Lang. "Because one lane was closed, they had traffic lights set up at each end. The only trouble was, you could be halfway across and the lights would change and cars would start coming toward you. That happened to me one night, and I had to crowd into the construction area to let them pass. That was why I hated the bridge, and why Lana and I were talking about it as we went along. Both of us said we knew somebody would be hurt there before long. It was just too dangerous."

As the two women travelled, neither knew that a gasoline truck was behind them, out of sight but rapidly drawing closer. The huge twenty-two-wheel, fifty-tonne Brunswick Petroleum transport was driven by thirty-four-year-old Charles Steeves, a trucker with fourteen years of accident-free experience behind him. The tanker carried 45,000 litres of gasoline.

In the meantime, on the bridge ahead, work was halted while the construction crew ate lunch. Several men had gone to their cars for sandwiches, or to the nearby Mandarin House restaurant for a hot meal. Only a handful of workers remained on the job. The time was 12:35 P.M.

As Anna eased her car around the long curve that leads down onto the western end of the bridge, she saw that the temporary traffic light facing her was green. At this point, though she didn't know it, Charles Steeves's gasoline tanker was less than twenty metres behind her.

Then the light turned red.

"When the red came on, I automatically stopped the car," explains Lang with a shudder. "Then I looked in the rearview mirror. All I could see were two headlights and a grille. Perhaps I saw the body of the truck but I can't remember it. The grille seemed to fill my whole back window and his horn was blaring and I was screaming: 'Oh God, Lana, he's not going to stop. He's not going to stop.' "

Up in the cab of his truck, Charles Steeves was terrified. He jammed on his brakes and sounded his horn. Yet he knew he could never stop in time. "My God," he thought to himself, "I'm going to kill them all."

The careering tanker smashed into the back of the Lang auto, demolishing the entire rear end and ramming the trunk against the front seat. In the same instant, the back window exploded inward and hundreds of jagged glass particles were driven into the interior of the car. Little Jaye Walsh was knocked flying into the front seat.

"When the back window popped, the glass made the inside of the car look like a cave with ice crystals hanging down," Lang recalls. "The ice kept coming until it covered the roof, the sides and even the dash. I remember being pushed forward and then crawling back to the seat again. My head hit the steering wheel and my glasses were thrown off.

Everything was so slow that it's still imprinted on my mind. It was as if you were watching a movie and all these things were happening at once — but they were barely moving. Lana was thrown around as much as I was."

Walsh was tossed screaming against the windshield, shattering it. At the same time, with a mother's instinct, she grabbed Jaye and held him to her. The possibility that he would be harmed bothered her far more than the thought of injury to herself.

The few remaining construction workers on the bridge froze at the sudden loud crash. However, a young man named Steve Hickey, who had been walking across with his three-year-old nephew Kevin, didn't even pause to see what was happening. He scooped the child off his feet and raced across the bridge and out of danger.

In desperation, Charles Steeves had tried to swing the huge truck to the left, into the narrow space between the Lang car and the side of the bridge. He had failed. As his truck telescoped the car, the two vehicles ploughed through black and yellow traffic barriers and construction equipment, and finally rammed the cement forms and steel reinforcing rods from which the new guardrails would be built.

"The impact of the crash tore the tires from my car," explains Lang. "Then there was a loud, grating, grinding sound, like a teacher scratching her nails across a blackboard — only a hundred times as loud. Sparks were flying and everyone was screaming and by this time the truck had jackknifed and we were still moving forward."

Two seconds later, both vehicles veered to the right and plunged into space.

"I tried my best to keep my truck on the bridge," Steeves said later. "I never dreamed we would both end up in the river. There was no guardrail, and when I saw that my truck was headed for the edge, I thought, 'I have to get out, she's going to blow.' I jumped at the last minute, and I could feel her starting to go when I jumped. I don't remember hitting the ground."

Jumping from his moving truck, Steeves fell headlong into a series of steel reinforcing bars that were imbedded upright in cement. Despite the fact that his side was badly lacerated and one of the rods was driven into his leg, he got to his feet and scrambled to safety, shouting at the workers to get off the bridge. Blood was spurting from his leg all the while.

Then the first explosion came.

Bystanders watched in utter horror as gasoline, ignited by flying sparks from the collision, shredded the steel of the truck like the burst of a bomb. A waterfall of fire poured from the bridge as the compartmentalized fuel bays were torn open, one after the other. As each exploded, the sound ricocheted along the river, shook buildings a kilometre away, and sent a tower of flame higher than the trees. This was followed by a pall of smoke that was seen from as far away as Saint John.

In the dining room of the Mandarin House restaurant, which looks out on the Hammond River bridge, a waitress was taking orders. Both she and the dining room patrons heard the collision, but none of them was prepared for the pillar of fire that roared up from the river below. "The waitress screamed and came running from the dining room," recalls Lily Yee, one of the restaurant's owners. "I

The burning tanker spews rings of flame across the surface of the Hammond River.

grabbed the phone and called the fire department. Then I yelled at my husband to get our papers and get out. I was afraid the whole place would burn. The customers left right away. They said they couldn't eat after what they had seen. We closed the place down for over an hour."

While all this was happening, Anna Lang's battered Buick hit the water, right side up.

"When we were being pushed along the bridge, there was so much racket," says Lang, "but when we went over the side my car seemed to spin around and I could see the restaurant. I knew it should have been behind me, though, and for a minute I had no idea where I was. I suppose the car was in the air at the time. Then I guess we went into the water. For a minute everything was silent and I can recall thinking, 'Oh God, it's all over.' Suddenly there was water in the car."

A moment later the transport tractor fell into the river on its roof, a metre away. Then the shattered tanker landed on its side, disgorging burning gasoline into the water in shimmering, scorching, deadly waves. Further explosions came, each adding more fuel to the wild inferno. The leaping, crackling, roaring flames obliterated all signs of life.

But there was life.

"My car sank right away," explains Lang, "and water started pouring in. I kept holding my breath until I thought my lungs would burst. The next thing I knew, Lana was holding Jaye and I was floating over them, out the right window. I remember hitting the surface and gasping for air, but the whole river was burning and I could hardly breathe. It was so hot.

"Because we had been to exercise class, both Lana and I had a lot more clothing on than we normally would have. I was wearing jeans and a couple of heavy sweaters over my tights and leotards. As soon as the jeans and sweaters got wet, they weighed a tonne so I knew I had to get rid of them if I was going to be any help to Lana and Jaye. By this time they had got to the surface, so I started swimming for shore.

"As I was swimming I was saying, 'Lana, I'll be back, I'll be back.' She never heard me say that and I never heard her say, 'Anna, please come back for me.' I guess we both thought these things but we never mouthed the words."

Now the fire was spreading farther and farther over the river. Rings of flame alternated with patches of clear water as Anna fought her way through the inferno toward shore, forty metres away. "I tried to duck under each ring and then get my breath in the clear spaces," she says, "but that was not always possible. It was so hot on top, I felt better if I stayed under. Then I remember getting to shore and trying very hard to quickly take my outer clothes off. When I finally got rid of them, I went back in."

While Anna was struggling with her wet clothes, Lana Walsh and Jaye were having difficulties in the water.

"I was trying to hold Jaye up," Lana said later. "We had gone down several times and I was getting tired. So tired. And the heat was unbearable. Everything was burning. My big sweater was pulling me down and I was getting so tired that I was starting to give up. I wanted to save Jaye, but the heat was so bad. Everything was burning and I had to keep pushing his head under the water. Then I looked and he wasn't moving, and I thought he was dead. But then his eyelids moved. The water was burning and Jaye's hair was on fire."

Jaye floated on his back and his mother held onto him with her left hand, keeping herself afloat with her right. When his hair began to burn, she would push him under to put the flames out.

"Then I saw Anna on the shore," Walsh says, "but she seemed so far away. I saw blood pouring down her face. She was taking off her jeans and sneakers, and I can see her now splashing into the water. She came back for us. The water was burning but she really came back for us."

"As soon as I couldn't feel the bottom anymore, I started swimming," recalls Lang. "I decided to grab Jaye instead of his mother because I was afraid she might panic and drown us all. I knew if I got Jaye, she would hold on. That's what happened. He had taken swimming lessons the winter

Whenever Anna's hair caught fire she ducked her head underwater to keep her hair from burning.

before and I think that's what saved him."

"I finally got to them," Lang adds, "and grabbed Jaye by the shoulder and started pulling both of them after me. Every so often my hair would go on fire and I had to keep ducking to put it out. I believe Lana was in too much shock to do that.

"As we got closer to the shore, everything seemed to be so quiet. Jaye was very quiet and so was Lana. I guess there were people up on the bridge watching, although I was not aware of it. I was just too busy."

But not everyone was on the bridge watching.

Two local teens, Eric Sparks and Jack Chaisson, both eighteen, had been in a car behind the gasoline tanker. They had witnessed the accident, but had been able to stop before becoming involved in it.

When they saw the vehicles plunge off the bridge, they left their car and made their way down the south embankment to the edge of the river. Almost without thinking, Sparks took off his pants and waded into the water to help with the rescue. By this time Anna was approaching the shore with Jaye and Lana in tow.

"There was still a lot of burning gas around us, but I could see those guys ahead of me," recalls Anna. "They were standing on the bank and one had no pants on. I remember thinking, Why is he in his underwear? when I saw him coming into the water. I kept saying, 'Please help me, God. I'm not going to make it.'

"Eric got to me just as my feet touched the bottom again. He grabbed Jaye and handed him to Jack and then he got Lana. They had to carry them because Lana wasn't able to walk. At this point, I didn't want

71

to look at her, or at Jaye. I didn't know what they looked like, if they were cut, had broken arms or anything. I didn't know what I had done to them."

Finally Anna managed to pull herself up onto the rocky shore, her head, face and neck now severely burned, her face bloody, and what was left of her clothes in tatters. She would not know until later that she had two cracked vertebrae in her back.

Even though they were now on shore, they were far from safe. Across the water the crackling flames engulfed more and more of the tanker, but still the flow of gasoline had not slowed.

"We've got to get out of here right away," Jack cried. "That thing is going to blow again."

He had no sooner said the words than the last of several explosions boomed across the water, spewing a geyser of steam, mud, flaming gasoline and hunks of shattered steel into the air. The earth shook and little Jaye clasped Jack Chaisson in a terrified but silent bear-hug. Eric knelt on the ground beside Lana, placed his arms under her back and legs and hoisted her into his arms. Anna, by now so exhausted she felt she would drop, wobbled unsteadily for a moment, then straggled along after the others, away from the flames. Steadily, painfully, doggedly, the group made its way along the rocky shore, crossed under the bridge and then, helped by several others including trucker Charles Steeves, managed to reach the top of the bank and safety.

The first ambulance arrived four minutes later.

* * *

Anna, Lana and Jaye were all hospitalized as a result of their ordeal. Anna's injuries were the most serious and she was incapacitated for the longest time. Her back healed on its own, but the third-degree burns to her face and head required skin grafting, plastic surgery and hair transplants. She was well enough, however, to fly to Ottawa two years later to receive her Cross of Valour — although she claims she did not deserve it.

Anna Lang and Lana Walsh are still friends. To this day neither feels safe crossing the Hammond River bridge.

Amedeo Garrammone

Up Against the Wall

Shortly after 10:00 P.M. on November 4, 1978, three young sailors finished their meal, left a tip on the table, paid their bill and stepped out into Gottingen Street in the north end of Halifax, Nova Scotia. Although the evening was cool, the fog and rain of earlier days had at least gone.

As the three friends waited for thc traffic to clear before they crossed the street to return to their barracks, they noticed a tall, sandy-haired, rather unkempt-looking young man standing in the shadows nearby. A woman was with him.

The man shouted something at the sailors, but they ignored him. "Hey, goof," he yelled, this time loudly and with a good deal of sarcastic belligerence. "Hey, goof, come here!" he repeated, glaring at eighteen-year-old Bradley Quinn from Hamilton, Ontario.

Brad Quinn turned.

Then the man slowly removed his jacket, handed it to the woman and walked over to Quinn.

Quinn didn't move.

The man snarled something else, positioned himself directly in front of Quinn and punched the young sailor in the face. The punch had hardly landed when Quinn decided he had taken enough. His right hand flashed. Then his left. Then his right again. His assailant cursed, tried to duck his head and finally crumpled in a heap on the pavement. The fight was over.

Stephen Holden, another of the navy men, stepped forward and took Quinn's shoulder. As he did so, the fallen man got to his feet and raced toward the Northend Beverage Room, a nearby hotel. The woman was left behind.

For a few seconds Holden, Quinn and James Hoy, the third sailor, stood and watched the man run. Then Hoy turned to cross the street, this time slightly ahead of his two friends. Quinn glanced in the direction of the hotel, but then, following some urging from Holden, shrugged his shoulders and started back toward the base.

James Hoy had just crossed the street when he heard a commotion in front of the hotel. He turned to look. Stuart "Skippy" Hamblin, the man who had hit Quinn, barged out of the hotel and into the street with two other men. Hamblin, an ex-convict who had just been released from prison after serving time for crimes of violence, was not about to lose face. He had been defeated and embarrassed in public, in a fight he had started, and now he wanted to get even. He and his friends paused for a second or two, then start to run toward Brad Quinn.

Quinn noticed them as well, but apparently decided he'd had enough fighting. He dashed toward the main entrance of Stadacona, the Halifax

Canadian Forces Base. As he did, he passed Amedeo Garrammone.

Earlier that evening, jovial twenty-three-year-old Garrammone, a champion weight-lifter in the Canadian military, had gone for a walk downtown. He was wearing a light shirt and slacks and a brown corduroy jacket. "The jacket was not particularly [warm]," he says today, "so when the evening started to get cooler, I decided to turn back to the base. As I was approaching Stadacona, I was walking fairly fast, but suddenly a tall young guy with short, dark hair raced past me. Three guys were chasing him.

"From the look of things, I was pretty sure there was going to be a fight," Garrammone recalls, "but I had no idea what it was about. I knew none of the people involved. From the way the first guy was running, though, I figured he would make it to the front gates of the base without getting caught. He was really flying."

While his friends watched from some distance away along the street, Brad Quinn steadily drew away from his pursuers. Two of them were already falling behind, and Skippy Hamblin was even farther back.

Suddenly Quinn's right foot came down on a loose stone on the sidewalk. He stumbled, then lurched sideways and fell face down on the cement. He had just got back on his feet when the two strangers reached him.

"The next thing I knew, they were both beating the fellow who ran past me," says Garrammone. "They were punching him and kicking him and he was up against a wall and couldn't get away. Then the third guy got there and he seemed to dance up

76

and down for a couple seconds, as if he was waiting his turn."

After the two men with Hamblin had delivered several blows, Hamblin apparently decided his chance had come. But instead of using his fists, or even his feet, he reached under his clothing and pulled out a knife. Then he lunged at Quinn with it.

"I saw him raise his left hand," Garrammone recounts, "and then I saw the blade flash for a second in the light from a streetlamp overhead. The hand came down again and again, and I knew the guy against the wall was being stabbed."

Garrammone stood transfixed for a second, not believing what he was seeing. The young sailor moaned in pain and vainly tried to protect himself. "No! No more. Please, no more," he cried, but Hamblin continued his insane assault.

Garrammone recovered his senses, yelled at the attackers and rushed to the scene.

"I really was hoping somebody would help me," he says today. "I looked across at the west side of Gottingen Street and thought I saw several sailors on the sidewalk in front of the hotel. One man started toward the fight, but he seemed to stop in the middle of the street.

"By the time I reached the location, the thug with the knife was really going at it. I yelled at him to stop and grabbed him by the shoulders.

"We scuffled for a few seconds and he was cursing me. Then he swung around and attacked me from the right. I tried to break the speed of his hand but I was not able to do so. The knife penetrated the right side of my chest and the tip went across and into my heart.

"At that time I straightened up and looked straight into his eyes, while the knife was still in my chest. We stayed like that for about two seconds, but then I seemed to become paralyzed and I couldn't carry on the fight any longer.

"When he pulled the blade out, blood gushed out of my chest and I put my hand over the wound. When the knife went in, I felt no physical pain, but as soon as it was out and I was losing blood, I started to lose strength."

As soon as he realized that Garrammone was out of action, Hamblin turned again to Quinn. He stabbed the fallen sailor three more times, but then was pulled off by his fellow attackers. "Let's go, Skippy!" shouted one of them, and the three dashed away. The whole incident lasted less than a minute.

While Quinn lay bleeding on the sidewalk, Amedeo Garrammone staggered toward the main gate at Stadacona, twenty metres away.

"Every move I made took a lot out of me," he

Amedeo Garrammone kept telling himself he didn't want to die.

winces, "but I kept telling myself I didn't want to die. An old man came toward me and asked what had happened. I don't know if I told him or not. At the main gate, the duty commissionaire looked at me but didn't seem to know what was wrong.

"I felt my knees becoming weak, and I was trying to tell him I had been stabbed and there was another man on the sidewalk, but not much sound was coming out of my throat. I felt that my tongue was going down my throat, choking me. I put one knee on the cement and bent over because the pain was burning in my chest, but I refused to fall until I could hold out no more. Finally, I guess I fell over.

"The next thing I knew, there seemed to be a lot of people running around me, shouting, and I was pointing at my mouth, trying to get somebody to give me air. Later, I was told that a military policeman put a ruler in my mouth and kept me from swallowing my tongue. I was sweating a cold sweat, and then everything was darkness."

By the time his horrified friends realized what had happened, Brad Quinn was lying on the sidewalk with eighteen stab wounds in his upper body. The two ran to Quinn's side and screamed for an ambulance. One of them attempted to pursue Hamblin, but thought better of it. The man was vicious and he still had the knife. Instead, they bent over their friend and tried to comfort him until help arrived.

An ambulance arrived quickly, but the medical officer who helped load Quinn noticed that his breathing was already forced. The trip to the hospital lasted ninety seconds, during which time ambulance personnel massaged the victim's chest and applied mouth-to-mouth resuscitation. The efforts were futile, however. Dr. John Hamilton, on duty at the base hospital that night, pronounced Brad Quinn dead two minutes after his arrival in Emergency.

Eight minutes passed from the time Garrammone was stabbed until the ambulance was able to return for him. During this time he lay on his back, bleeding profusely and fighting to stay alive. A small crowd gathered, but the military and city police moved the curious onlookers away from the scene. The police also began to record names of witnesses to the stabbings. One name they obtained was that of Antonio LaChance, a Halifax taxi driver.

As the assailants were first running after Quinn, LaChance had been parking his taxi across the street. He saw the chase, and he also saw Hamblin using the knife to stab Quinn. When Hamblin fled, the cab driver followed in his car. A block away from the scene of the murder, LaChance caught sight of Hamblin, who was walking swiftly down a side street. As LaChance approached from the rear, he noticed that Hamblin still had the knife.

The cab driver lowered a window and yelled at Hamblin. Hamblin cursed, ducked behind the cab and disappeared down an alley. As soon as he realized he had lost his quarry, LaChance swung his vehicle around and went to report what he had seen to the police. In the meantime, ambulance attendants were wheeling Garrammone into the hospital where Brad Quinn had just died.

"I remember opening my eyes at the hospital," Garrammone says today. "I saw the ceiling in the emergency ward, but not much else. I asked a nurse about the man who was stabbed and she told me he had passed away. Then I gave somebody my girl-friend's phone number and I told them to call her. My own family wasn't in Halifax, and I didn't want them to know I was in the hospital. I knew they would worry."

Garramone was rushed into surgery. "During the operation I remember fighting hard to stay alive because I was somehow aware that something was going wrong. I felt as though my head was diving in one direction and my feet were going the other way — and at that time I could hear a lot of noise in the room.

"Then I became very frightened and I wanted to scream, but I was terribly tired and I couldn't move. I never felt so bad in all my life. That was when I decided to let myself go. As soon as I did, I felt no more fear but felt warm and good. There were lots of lights. When I woke up later in intensive care, I was actually kind of disappointed. I can't explain why."

Amedeo Garrammone was born in Belgium, the son of an Italian coal miner who also sang opera. There are seven children in the family, and at the time of the Halifax stabbing, the family was living in Montreal. Both parents speak Italian and French.

"The Roman Catholic padre contacted my parents," says Garrammone now. "They flew to Halifax, and my girlfriend, Eve Galley, met them. She had never seen them before, and when they arrived she had to hold up a sign at the airport with my name on it. They came over to her, of course, but because she couldn't speak their languages, she couldn't tell them if I was alive or dead. She took my mother's hand and squeezed it, and they drove to the hospital in silence."

* * *

Amedeo Garrammone was in the hospital for three weeks and off work for two months. His assailant, Stuart Hamblin, was apprehended by the Halifax police and charged with the second-degree murder of Brad Quinn. After a six-day trial that saw a total of twenty-nine witnesses take the stand, an all-male jury found the defendant guilty as charged. He was sent to prison for life.

Gaston Langelier

Escape!

Laval Maximum Security Institution, just north of Montreal, houses some of the most notorious criminals in Canada. Here, in the sprawling, granite fortress that was once called St. Vincent de Paul Penitentiary, 500 men live, work, sleep and dream of being free. Few of them are pleasant people, and all are here because they have broken the law.

The prison was built more than a hundred years ago and received its first inmates on May 20, 1873. Since then it has been enlarged, modernized, renamed, but rarely praised. Indeed, the complex has been found wanting during most of its infamous history. In 1973 it was condemned and closed, but a short while later had to be reopened because of a rise in the prison population.

Over the years a number of convicts have escaped from Laval. Some were away for a few hours, others for a few days. Most were recaptured eventually. Still, the knowledge that escapees are usually caught did not deter the five men planning their own escape for the early afternoon of Tuesday, July 11, 1978.

The five, Jacques Massey, Pierre Vincent, André Chartrand, Ghislain Gaudette and Jean Lachapelle were serving time for either armed robbery or murder. All had been in the prison for some time, and all were considered dangerous. One of the five, Vincent, had escaped several times from several jails.

At 1:00 P.M. on the day of the escape, the electronically operated steel doors from the cell blocks swung open to permit the inmates to enter the cavernous central square, or "dome," of Laval. From here, the prisoners moved to various other locations within the penitentiary itself. Some reported for work. Others went to see lawyers. Some had

Laval Maximum Security Prison houses some of the most notorious criminals in Canada.

visitors, and as always, a few reported to the medical ward. The five men who planned to escape carried written passes to see prison officials. These passes were forged.

The five proceeded separately through the dome, across the paved prison grounds toward the guarded entrance to the two-storey administration wing of the jail. This 200-metre walk was witnessed by armed guards on duty in the observation towers, high above the prison walls. None of them noticed anything amiss.

The five came together at the entrance to the administration wing. The first two showed their passes to Richard Rolland, a security guard inside a steel-reinforced control booth just outside the administration vestibule. Rolland checked the passes and signalled to Marc Drouin, a second guard stationed in the vestibule, to open the door to permit the two inmates to enter.

The first part of the escape plan was working.

The door was hardly open before all five convicts charged through it. Drouin stumbled backward in surprise, and the next thing he knew, both he and a male nurse who happened to be with him were forced against the opposite wall by the inmates holding deadly, sharpened stilettos or "pics."

One of the convicts told Drouin and the nurse to do as they were told and they would not be harmed. Another, Jacques Massey, reached into his trousers pocket and produced a small .25 calibre handgun that had been smuggled into the prison. He pointed the weapon at Rolland and ordered him to open the security cage and hand out a revolver and a shotgun that were inside.

Rolland refused.

Massey flew into a rage, pushed his pistol through a small opening into the control booth and fired three shots, the first of which passed through Rolland's body, wounding him seriously. The other two shots hit the corner of a desk and the arm of the chair where Rolland had been sitting. Despite his injuries, the guard managed to drag himself under his desk, out of the line of fire. Because of his wounds, he was unable to do anything further to impede the escape.

The volley of shots seemed to drive all five prisoners into a frenzy. Because they had been frustrated in their attempts to obtain more weapons, they turned to the guard, Marc Drouin, ripped his keys from his belt and managed to open the door that led from the vestibule into the second-floor office area. Massey then grabbed Drouin by the collar, jammed the pistol into the small of his back and ordered him to co-operate. Drouin realized that he was being used as a shield and expected to be shot if the escape attempt was interrupted. He did as he was told. The male nurse was left in the vestibule.

There are several offices and some thirty doorways leading off the long hallway on the second floor of the administration wing. Halfway down the hall is a sliding steel grille barrier that can be secured to prevent escape. One of the escapees raced down the hall and propped a chair into the open barrier to keep it from closing. Three others went from office to office, using the pics to threaten people and ordering everyone they found into the hall. Massey held his gun on Marc Drouin.

As each office was vacated, the crowd of terrified

hostages grew larger. The inmates screamed at everyone to hurry, and the grim procession moved swiftly toward the large conference room and adjoining stairs leading down to the main entrance of the prison.

Just before the stairs, on the left, is the office of the assistant director of security. At the time of the escape, this person was Gaston Langelier.

"I had been in the correctional service for twenty-three years," he recalls, "and at Laval for three. I had experience with other escapes, but this one was by far the most serious for me.

"I was sitting at my desk when I heard some racket in the hall outside. The next thing I knew, inmate Massey barged into my office, put his revolver up to my head and ordered me out into the corridor. By this time, there were twenty or thirty people there. I did what he asked."

While this was happening, one of the hostages, who was ahead of the others, raced down the stairs and passed through a swing-open grille barrier at the bottom. He yelled for the front door of the prison to be opened because he feared for the lives of the hostages who were coming behind him. Already some of them were at the top of the stairs.

The first person to hear the plea was twenty-seven-year-old Guy Fournier, a guard on duty at the main desk. He immediately ran to investigate. As he got to the grille barrier, he was met by several fleeing employees. Fournier jumped to the side and the crowd swept past. He glanced up the stairs, just as Gaston Langelier and another officer, Marcel Boucher, were coming down. Behind the two was an inmate with a gun.

"I was on the left side, facing down," says Langelier. "Marcel Boucher was on my right and Jacques Massey was walking behind us. At this time Massey had the gun in the back of Mr. Boucher and was pushing me with his hand. Then, out of the corner of my eye, I noticed the inmate make a move to take the revolver with his other hand. That was when I went for him."

Suddenly Langelier spun around, grabbed Massey by the arm and twisted it up behind the convict's back. The inmate cursed, ducked his head and lurched across the stairs. The gun clattered onto the terrazzo steps and the two men fell, both wildly grasping for the weapon. At this point there was a lot of shouting and Langelier and Massey tumbled to the bottom of the stairs. As he fell, Langelier shouted for the barrier to be closed.

For a split second, the gun lay by itself.

Guard Guy Fournier saw it first. He dashed to retrieve it, but inmate Lachapelle was quicker. He grabbed the weapon, brought it up to chest level and fired one shot. Fournier was hit in the forehead and died within seconds. Marc Drouin, the twenty-one-year-old guard who had been the first hostage taken, lunged at Lachapelle, apparently to stop him from shooting at Fournier. Instead the inmate turned to face the young guard and fired a second time. The bullet ripped into Drouin's jaw, spun him around and caused him to fall down the stairs. Later he was able to get to his feet and leave with the last of the hostages.

"As the two shots rang out, there was a great deal of shouting and screaming," Gaston Langelier remembers. "Then I could see that another officer

"The next thing I knew, inmate Massey barged into my office, put his revolver up to my head and ordered me out into the corridor."

at the control post by the main entrance was trying to hand me a gun. I guess Lachapelle saw the same thing, because he came over and took charge of me. He had his gun in my back and then he started screaming at somebody to open the front door or there would be a massacre."

While Langelier was being held by Lachapelle with the gun, guard Boucher and others were threatened by the convicts holding the sharpened pics. The situation just inside the front doors was becoming more frenzied, with much screaming, shoving and crying. Finally someone ordered the door to the main lobby opened.

As soon as the pressure was off, a torrent of terrified people poured through. Both employees and convicts raced for the exit, and once through it, fled in panic away from the deadly chaos at the foot of the stairs.

"There were people all over the place," says Langelier. "Convicts, visitors who were there to see inmates, other hostages. . . . Then, when the doors opened, everyone tried to get out at once — including Lachapelle and the other inmates.

"As soon as he saw the open door, Lachapelle forgot about me, but I grabbed him because I was determined he was not going to get away."

The prisoner raised his weapon and fired twice. Both shots hit Langelier on the right side of his face and propelled him across the room toward the control post at the front entrance.

"I knew he was going to shoot again," says Langelier with a shudder, "and I was sure I was going to be killed. But then I saw the door guard push the .38 toward me through the small opening in his control post. As I was about to grab the gun to defend myself, another bullet broke my arm. I kept going, something like the walking dead. I knew I was bleeding a lot because I saw my reflection in the control-post glass. Blood was spurting from my ear.

"Anyway, I finally managed to grab the revolver, and when I turned around, Lachapelle was shooting at me from across the room. I fired back and he shot again and again — from three metres away. I felt as though I was dying, and then I saw him fall. He died in the lobby.

"Somehow I kept going. I handed the gun back and walked on my own to another room called the Keeper's Hall. As soon as I got there, they put me on a couch and called an ambulance. They also gave me the last rites."

In the meantime, on the floor above, a woman who had been in a washroom during the roundup of the hostages crept from her hiding place and glanced down the corridor toward the stairs. When she knew she was out of sight, she darted into her office and phoned guards in the dome and towers to alert them of the escape in progress. Other areas of the prison were immediately secured.

By this time the escapees had left Lachapelle behind and were out the front door. They extricated themselves from the mob of panic-stricken employees, raced across the jail parking lot and surrounded a red Toyota that had just pulled onto the property.

One of the convicts yelled at the driver, Jean Vigneault, pushed him into the back seat and placed a pic against his neck. Then the other three climbed into the little car, rammed it into gear and raced across a front lawn and off the property. As they sped north on Montée St-François, shots rang out from the towers atop the prison, but none was accurate. Vigneault was later released unharmed.

* * *

In the aftermath of the bloody daylight escape, two men were dead — a guard and a convict. Three other guards were injured, but all of them, including Gaston Langelier, recovered successfully. Marc Drouin, the first hostage, and Guy Fournier, the murdered guard, were both awarded the Star of Courage, the nation's second-highest award for bravery. Eight months after the incident, Gaston Langelier received the Cross of Valour.

All the escapees were subsequently captured.

Sceviour, Miller and Fudge

Trapped in the Ice!

The sea was calm at daybreak, but by noon the weather had closed in and the horizon had disappeared. Sheets of freezing rain, swept by a wild north wind, lashed the vessel toiling in the chilling wastes of the North Atlantic. The ship strained in the storm. The screws plunged in the troughs between the waves, then screamed in the air when the stern was heaved above the surface. By mid-afternoon what little ceiling existed under the low clouds seemed to disappear. The boiling ocean tossed the *Remoy* like a cork.

The Danish trawler had been in the area for days, fishing for shrimp along the northern coast of Labrador. Ordinarily, hundreds of islands, most of them barren rock, had provided a measure of protection from the rolling sea, but on this Sunday — November 19, 1978 — the frigid gales gave no quarter. The *Remoy* was in danger. Twenty-nine-year-old Captain Ulf Snarby knew it, and so did the crew of eleven who were with him.

He decided to head for port.

The journey was not easy. At times, when her bow nosed downward into a long, rolling breaker, it seemed as if the *Remoy* would never right herself. But each time, slowly, fitfully, the bow would rise and a torrent of half-frozen sea ice would wash from the decks. Each man on board braced himself against the ship's rolling.

In the wheelhouse the strength of the storm was even more obvious than elsewhere. Because it is above the rest of the ship, the wheelhouse moves farther with every roll. Many of the hands fought down the queasiness and nausea that only those who have sailed rough seas can know.

During this November gale there was little that could be seen. The sea was just too rough, and the wind-driven rain obscured anything more than 100 metres beyond the boat. Because they knew they could not see anything if they went outside, most crew members congregated below decks, in the galley. There they chatted about the storm, nursed cups of hot coffee and wondered how long it might take the *Remoy* to reach Nain, the little Labrador port where they would wait for better weather. Some felt they would be in harbour by nightfall; others believed the journey would take much longer than that. A few wondered if they would get there at all.

In the early afternoon, the shrieking winds occa- sionally abated, and when they did, the ocean seemed calmer. But with the approach of dark- ness, the wind picked up to 100 km/h, the temperature dropped to -25°C, and gusts of freezing rain and snow pelted the vessel.

The men in the galley braced themselves against the pitching of the ship and continued their small talk. But with each passing minute they found it harder and harder to think of anything but the storm. In the wheelhouse the lurching motion of the *Remoy* was so violent no one could stand without support. A pair of binoculars placed on a shelf remained where they were for only a second before they crashed to the floor and slid across the room.

Ship navigation in the Labrador Sea is not easy at the best of times, but on this wild November afternoon it had become almost impossible. The charts on board all indicated water depth and safe channels, but the roaring seas made it harder and harder for the *Remoy* to stay on course. This was particularly true as Captain Snarby headed into the long, winding Strathcona Run, the channel that led to Nain. Here the hundreds of shoals and craggy islands, and the pounding surf, were a mariner's nightmare.

But Ulf Snarby had a more serious problem.

The waves that washed across the decks of the *Remoy* had become a dangerous threat. The sea ports at the stern of the ship, small doors that automatically opened and closed to let the water run off the deck, had frozen open. Sea water rushed in, and in the intense cold froze on the deck, layer upon layer. The heavy ice was beginning to make the ship list to port.

At first barely noticeable, the list soon became more and more pronounced. Snarby ordered his men to free the valves controlling the sea ports, but the task was impossible. Propping the ports shut did not work either: each time a wave sloshed over the deck, the props were torn loose. The port side of the ship sank lower and lower in the water.

Captain Snarby knew the *Remoy* would capsize unless something was done — and soon. He began to sail a sharp zigzag course in the hope that the wrenching of the ship from side to side might unclog the ports and enable some of the water on the stern section of the deck to drain. The manoeuvre failed. As he stood in the wheelhouse wondering what else he could do to remove the water from the deck, the radar screen in front of him suddenly went blank. The small engines that drove the scanners had frozen.

By this time, night had come. Ulf Snarby decided to call for help.

While all this was happening, several other trawlers had successfully navigated the Strathcona Run and reached Nain. Two of these were the *Zaragoza* and the *Zermatt*. One man working on the *Zaragoza* was twenty-nine-year-old Martin Sceviour.

"When we heard Goose Bay radio issuing storm warnings, we headed for Nain," recalls Sceviour today. "Most of the shrimp fleet came in at this time. Then some of us went to the Atsanik Lodge to wait until the weather got better. We had been fishing about sixty kilometres out of Nain, but by late that Sunday afternoon we had been in port for four hours or so."

Only one ship, far out at sea, heard Ulf Snarby radio his S.O.S. Fortunately, that vessel was able to contact a receiving station in Hopedale, a tiny Labrador community 150 kilometres south of Nain.

But even though the message was now on the coast, transmission troubles caused a delay of two hours before the call for help got to Nain. As the radio operator in Hopedale attempted to reach Nain, he learned to his dismay that his base transmission tower had been flattened by the storm. Nevertheless, the plea for assistance eventually got through.

"The RCMP came to the lodge and told us there was a ship in trouble," recounts Harold Miller, then twenty, also with the *Zaragoza*. "The *Zermatt* went out to see what could be done. Neither Martin Sceviour nor I was on board at this time."

The RCMP lent a motor boat to the *Zermatt* for the trip. The small outboard was hauled onto the trawler, and the rescue mission began.

By this time, the problem-plagued *Remoy* was aground. Once he found that his ship was on the verge of capsizing and his radar had gone, Ulf

Snarby forced his ship aground on this rugged coast to prevent it from capsizing.

Snarby had decided to take his ship in to the nearest island and deliberately force her aground. He reasoned that both he and his men would have a greater chance of survival if they were closer to land.

The *Remoy* came to rest on a sand bottom. But the surf crashing on surrounding rocks would mean certain death to anyone foolhardy enough to try to paddle to shore. A rubber raft lowered into the sea was swamped in seconds. The dinghy was hauled back on board and captain and crew prepared themselves for a long wait for rescue — if it came at all.

It took the *Zermatt* about an hour and a half to reach the crippled *Remoy*, and when the rescuers saw where the forty-metre trawler was aground, they were amazed that she had not been torn apart among the rocks. Giant breakers crashed over the grounded vessel, and the ice that coated her was getting thicker and heavier with every minute that passed. On one side the deck was almost level with the sea.

Captain Kirk Mitchell of the *Zermatt* took his ship close to the *Remoy* — too close. Without warning, the *Zermatt* hit a sandbar and shuddered to a stop. Mitchell immediately ordered the engines reversed and the *Zermatt* slowly backed toward deeper water, 300 metres from shore.

Just then the emergency lights on the *Remoy* went out. The Danish trawler was now little more than an ice-coated hulk in the storm. But, hulk or not, there were still a dozen worried men on board.

Captain Mitchell again eased the fifty-metre *Zermatt* as close as he dared to the *Remoy*. He ordered a powerful searchlight on board his ship to be directed at the vessel on the rocks. Then, with the light as their guide, men on the *Zermatt* fired rocket lines toward the *Remoy,* in the hope of rigging a line between the ships. The wild wind tossed the rockets into the sea. The men tried to launch a lifeboat, but it sank almost as soon as it hit the water. The time now was 11:30 P.M.

On the *Remoy,* the stranded fishermen despaired as each rescue attempt failed. They were now without light or heat; their stricken ship was almost entirely covered with ice, and they knew that at any minute the pounding waves might tear their boat apart. If that happened, even the best swimmer would not survive. Not only was the sea violent, but the terrible cold would kill a man in minutes.

Someone mentioned that the *Zermatt's* lights seemed to be farther away. Several men peered into the blackness and scoffed at the suggestion that the rescue boat would back off. But the lights of the *Zermatt* did become fainter and finally disappeared entirely. The rescuers were gone!

The crew of the *Remoy* wondered, but they had not been abandoned. Kirk Mitchell had already sent a radio message to the RCMP in Nain, asking them to locate another boat that could be launched from the *Zermatt.* Mitchell said he would be back in port in an hour and a half.

"When word got around that the first rescue was a failure — that they were going out again — Harold Miller and I volunteered to go," says Martin Sceviour. "The RCMP borrowed a boat from some of the Inuit in Nain, and Harold and I took it out to meet the *Zermatt.*

"It was a fibreglass speedboat, about six metres long. It had a little cabin in the middle, but you steered it at the back.

"We had no trouble getting it on board the *Zermatt,* but the trip back out to the *Remoy* took another hour and a half. As we were going out I found myself wondering about the safety of the guys we were going to rescue — whether we would get to them before their boat sank or they froze to death."

The *Zermatt* anchored about a kilometre from the shoal where the *Remoy* lay. Between the ships the frightening gale blew the crests from wavetops, lashing with spray the men who struggled to drop the speedboat into the water. Even the Zermatt, which now carried some twenty-three men, lurched up and down like a rodeo rider on horseback. The time was 2:00 A.M.

The speedboat was lowered over the side. It stayed afloat. In the garish floodlight from the trawler, the drenched fishermen on deck held firmly to a line hooked to the speedboat's bow. But just as Lester Fudge, the first mate of the *Zermatt,* was about to go down into the outboard, a freezing breaker crashed against her and she filled with water.

The *Zermatt* crew hauled the speedboat back on board, dumped the icy water out and hurriedly removed and dried the motor. Finally the little vessel was relaunched, with a line still hooked to the *Zermatt* in case the sea proved to be too rough. Lester Fudge, Martin Sceviour and Harold Miller volunteered to attempt the rescue. Fudge drove the boat and Miller bailed water out of it, while

Sceviour stood in front of the cabin, held on for dear life, and directed Fudge toward the *Remoy*. The wild ocean winds and the freezing spray made it impossible for Fudge to see much past the little cabin. From his position in the stern of the outboard, he yelled up to the *Zermatt* crew to let the rope out slowly, in case the speedboat swamped.

"The three of us felt better because that line was there," recalls Miller today. "But then something went wrong and they had to cut the rope. From then on we were left to look after ourselves. I remember being very tense as we started on that first trip over to the *Remoy*. I had to bail all the way."

To the three men in the outboard, the seas were like mountains. Huge breakers rolled over the six-metre craft, tossed it toward the black and rainy sky, then dropped it so far between the waves that

Fudge, Miller and Sceviour made repeated trips through the lashing storm to take the stranded men off the Remoy.

every minute or so neither the *Remoy* nor the *Zermatt* could be seen. On all sides, floating masses of half-formed ice slowed the boat, straining the already overworked motor.

But finally the rescuers reached the ice-covered *Remoy*.

As he drew in close to the stricken shrimp boat, Les Fudge decided to use the rubber raft from the *Remoy* as a kind of bumper. Once the dinghy was in position, Sceviour tossed a line toward the *Remoy*.

Almost as soon as the line was taut the *Remoy* crew prepared to abandon ship.

"We can't take you all at once," yelled Fudge. "We'll have to make two trips. Come on now, one at a time, jump!"

The first man clambered down to the speedboat. Six others followed in less than a minute.

"Okay, that's all for now," hollered Fudge. "We don't want to sink this thing. We'll be back."

With that, Sceviour pulled the line back in, Fudge reversed the motor and the tiny outboard backed out into the night. Harold Miller bailed for all he was worth.

The journey back to the *Zermatt* was worse than the trip out. With ten men on board, the motor boat was precariously low in the water. Often the sea was only a few centimetres from the gunwales, and to Miller it seemed as if every second wave washed over them. Yet somehow, after almost forty minutes defying the elements, Fudge eased in beside the *Zermatt* and seven grateful men climbed aboard her.

Fudge, Miller and Sceviour once again headed into the storm. An hour later they returned with the last of the men from the *Remoy*.

Captain Mitchell ordered the speedboat brought on board. Then he weighed anchor and headed for Nain. The rescue was completed — almost eleven hours after the *Remoy* had run aground.

* * *

The *Remoy* was pumped out, hauled off the shoal and towed into port for repairs. Then she returned to the sea that had almost claimed her.

After resting for a few hours, Lester Fudge, Martin Sceviour and Harold Miller helped chop ice from the trawlers. A day later, they returned to sea. On April 6, 1981, all three stood in front of the Governor General of Canada to receive the Cross of Valour.

Tom Hynes

"I'll die a hero."

The Burin Peninsula is a narrow, sparsely populated, sometimes lonely strip of land jutting into the sea from the south coast of Newfoundland. One can drive for great distances and never see a fence, a farm, or in some areas, even a tree. In the summer, warm breezes caress this wild land and make it beautiful. In winter, biting gales sweep in from the ocean and the barren plains become as desolate as the surface of the moon.

Most settlements on the peninsula are situated right by the sea. One of these is Jacques Fontaine, an attractive fishing village on Fortune Bay. Here, set amid weathered hills stretching back from the shore, are boat houses, clusters of well-kept homes, a modern high school, a post office and a cemetery. In that cemetery is the grave of Thomas Hynes, the youngest recipient of the Cross of Valour.

Not long before graduating from Jacques Fontaine High School, Tom told his friends he would die a hero.

"Yes, that is what he said to them," his mother, Martha Hynes, recalls. "And even when they laughed at him, he stuck to his story. He told them just to wait, that his name would be in the papers. In the grade eleven yearbook at school he said that his plans for the future were unknown. Maybe he knew he didn't have a future. He often said he would never marry. He didn't have a girlfriend."

The death of Tom Hynes is well remembered in Jacques Fontaine, but so is his life. He lived there for virtually all of his nineteen years, and he was as much a part of the village as the parish church is. With his rather shy manner, his shock of thick brown hair and his ready smile, he was welcome in every home. He played hockey, loved it and was good at it, but he also enjoyed driving his old snowmobile, one of the few things he ever owned. He never had much money, nor, for that matter, did anyone in his family.

"My late husband was a fisherman," says Mrs. Hynes, "and because there were fourteen in the family, we always had to struggle to make ends meet. We had four daughters and ten sons, and Tom was our sixth child. He was such a happy boy, always kidding and joking and making other people laugh. That was why everybody was so shocked when he died. I think of him every day, and of course I will never forget the day he died."

The day Martha Hynes remembers so vividly was December 29, 1977. It was the day Tom left the house for the last time. "That morning he had gone out to the post office and had taken his hockey equipment with him," she continues. "I assumed I was going somewhere to play hockey. But then he came back, left his hockey stuff here and went out again. I didn't know where he was going."

Around the time Tom was returning home with his hockey equipment, some neighbourhood boys on their Christmas holidays were playing along the shore of a partially frozen pond. The day was sunny and cold and they decided to test the ice. A day or so earlier it had not been hard enough to support them, but today might be different.

They gingerly eased out onto the surface of the pond. Air bubbles ran every which way under the ice and it began to crack, so everyone knew it was still not hard enough for hockey. With that, two of

This placid-looking pond became a death trap when Tom Hynes tried to cross its partially frozen surface to save two younger boys.

the boys, Wade Hynes, Tom's twelve-year-old brother, and his cousin Keith Hynes, age eight, started to search along the shoreline for pucks lost the previous winter.

The two plodded through the underbrush, talking and laughing as they went. Once or twice they stopped to toss bits of wood out onto the pond and watch as they skittered across the frozen surface. Then they noticed Tom standing on the far shore. Impetuously and with little thought to the danger, the two boys decided to cross the ice to see him. The fact that he was older and popular with every-one made them want to be with him.

Wade went first, walking slowly a step or two in front of Keith. The younger boy was slightly to one side. Tom watched from the far bank. The ice held.

The two boys went farther and farther, gliding their heavy winter overshoes along the slick sur-face. Through the ice near the shore they could see large rocks on the bottom, and long silky patches of weeds growing almost to the surface. But as they moved closer to the centre of the pond the water became deeper and the bottom disappeared, and both boys felt afraid.

Suddenly, with a loud cracking sound like a tree breaking in a storm, the ice started to give way.

Wade sensed the danger first and shouted a warning to Keith before spinning around and rac-ing for the nearest shore. The boys who were watching had never seen him move so fast, and they cheered when he touched land.

But the cheers did not last.

Out on the pond they saw Keith hesitate for a sec-ond, then move toward the opposite shore. He went cautiously at first, as if confused, but then dashed toward a point of land thirty metres away.

He did not get there. The echoes of ice cracking swept the surface of the pond, and before he had gone half a dozen steps, Keith lost his footing and plunged into the frigid water.

"I was really scared," he admits now. "I began to scream, because I didn't know how deep it was. I was also very cold. I remember holding onto the ice and trying to get myself up on it, but I kept slipping off. My clothes were heavy in the water and I couldn't get a grip on anything. I guess everybody was watching me, but I didn't think of that at the time."

Tom Hynes had been watching, and almost before Keith knew what had happened, his cousin was out onto the ice trying to help.

"He came toward me, but the ice broke under him too," Keith remembers. "I knew he would still try to come for me and he did."

As Keith floundered in the deep water, Tom eased closer and closer to him, half swimming and half supporting himself by grabbing at the edge of a large sheet of floating ice. He told Keith that he would be all right, and urged him to stay close to the ice sheet.

The younger boy did as he was told, but continued to scream in terror as the cold water soaked through his clothes, poured into his overshoes and pulled him down.

"Then Tom got under me and started pushing me up," says Keith. "But I couldn't get a grip on anything and I kept slipping. I know if he had not been there I would have died. I was cold and scared."

While the grim struggle went on in the centre of the pond, Wade and his friends looked on in desperation, wanting to help but not really knowing what to do. Once or twice one of them started out on the ice, but each time it cracked so much they retreated. Finally, somebody found a long wooden stake half-hidden by dead grass and scrubby pine boughs. The boys pulled the length of wood free and carried it to the shore.

Then the oldest of the group, fourteen-year-old Leo Farrell, slid the stake onto the ice and slowly crawled out toward Keith and Tom, while another boy ran for help.

In the meantime, Keith and Tom continued to flounder near the centre of the pond. With tears streaming down his face, his features constricted by fear, and his voice hoarse from screaming, Keith fought to hold on. He had slipped down several times, but each time Tom dived below the surface, grabbed him and pushed him back to the ice edge. Finally Tom managed to push Keith half out of the water so that the upper part of the younger boy's body rested on the ice.

"I can't remember whether Tom was still saying anything to me or not," says Keith. "All I know is that when he pushed me up, I didn't know he was in trouble himself."

But Tom Hynes *was* in trouble. He laboured almost mechanically, his effort and the numbing cold making him more exhausted with each second that passed. He dived one last time and pushed Keith as high as possible. Then, too tired to struggle anymore, he lost his grip and slipped beneath the ice.

Tom had told his friends at school that he would die a hero.

Although the onlookers did not realize it, Tom Hynes was dying.

About 100 metres away, Keith's mother was working in the kitchen when she heard screams at the door. "I don't remember which of the kids was there," Zita Hynes says today. "I just know that when I heard the word 'ice' I panicked. I never even thought of a coat. I just headed for the pond."

It took Zita less than a minute to run from her house to the little path that leads down to the pond — but she was already too late to save Tom.

"When I got there, I saw Leo kneeling on the ice, with Keith holding on to the end of a wooden stake. I never saw poor old Tom. I didn't even know he was there. I saw Keith's cap out there, but I never saw Tom at all.

"Leo stayed where he was, and Keith held on until somebody came with a rope and they were able to pull him out. But then, as soon as they got Keith to the shore, Wade and the others were yelling about Tom being gone. I really didn't know what they meant because I saw nothing of him. At the time I was just so grateful that Keith was safe."

Not long after Keith was pulled from the pond, the telephone rang at the Royal Canadian Mounted Police detachment in Burin, seventy-five kilometres to the south. Constable Fabian Sutton took the call. "I had only been at the detachment for three weeks or so, and I was still not too familiar with the area," recalls Sutton. "So Sergeant Conrad went with me to the scene of the accident. It's a fairly long drive, and by the time we got there, neighbours had recovered the body and the local parish priest had notified the next of kin."

Martha Hynes recalls how she was told of her son's death: "I heard somebody at the door, and when I opened it, Father Kevin Bennet was standing there. Before he even opened his mouth, I said 'Tom's dead, isn't he?' I don't know how I knew, I just knew."

The priest stood there for a second and then quietly nodded his head.

Tom Hynes was only nineteen when he died, but he died a hero — just as he said he would.

Ken Bishop

"I couldn't just let him die."

On the second last day of March, 1974, forty-three-year-old James McAdie was driving a fully loaded fuel truck east along Highway 16 in central Alberta. Hooked behind his rig was a pup trailer, also loaded. The weather was mild, the arrow-straight road was dry, and McAdie's spirits were as bright as the sun that shone overhead.

Despite the fairly heavy Saturday traffic out of Edmonton, he was making good time, and at 1:45 P.M. was about fifteen kilometres west of the Ukrainian settlement of Vegreville. As he hauled his 55,000 litres of diesel fuel across the prairie, he looked out at the snow-covered fields, dazzling in their brilliance. The hum of tires on blacktop was pleasant, and the vehicle he drove was working well. At least, it had been working well. Up ahead, perhaps half a kilometre away, he noticed another truck coming toward him.

The approaching transport, carrying twenty tonnes of flour, was driven by Robert Warren Hunter, twenty-five, of Saskatoon. A short distance behind Hunter's semi-trailer was a pickup truck carrying three people: nineteen-year-old Leslie Ferguson from Innisfail, Alberta, and Kay Green and her daughter Janice, who lived in nearby Vegreville.

Following the pickup were several vehicles, spaced at various distances, stretching back halfway to Vegreville. Somewhere in the midst of these was a car driven by twenty-eight-year-old Ken Bishop, a soft-spoken, rather reserved young man who resided at the time in Lloydminster, on the Alberta-Saskatchewan border. Ken Bishop also drove trucks for a living.

The traffic was moving at a constant speed, as if no one was in a hurry to be somewhere else. Few drivers attempted to pass.

Up in the cab of his oil tanker, Jim McAdie glanced at his watch and reasoned that he would be in Vegreville before 2:00 P.M. From there, the road was good; there were no hills and few curves all the way to the Saskatchewan border. The highway itself was two-lane, seven metres across, with wide, shallow ditches. Just beyond the north ditch was a railway.

As McAdie's glance shifted back to the road in front of him, he saw that the approaching transport was less than 100 metres away. He flashed his headlights and the other driver returned the greeting. As they were about to meet, both drivers waved.

That wave was Bob Hunter's last.

Suddenly, and without any warning, the steering mechanism on the fuel tanker broke. Jim McAdie grabbed the wheel and wrenched it to one side, but the instrument spun in his hands. His truck was out of control!

The huge, powerful vehicles came closer and closer together. McAdie automatically tramped his brakes and in the same instant hit the horn. The truck was veering to the left.

Bob Hunter gaped in open-mouthed horror as the speeding tanker roared down on him, its front end two metres across the centre line of the road. He yanked his steering wheel to the right in a desperate attempt to avoid a crash. He did not have time to use his brakes. The last thing he must have seen was the grille of the truck that would kill him.

A split second later, it happened.

With a sickening roar the vehicles tore into each other, sending an ear-splitting crash echoing across the snowswept plains. Metal tore like paper. The big, labouring diesel engines broke apart like bowling pins. Broken glass, chunks of plastic, rubber and steel flew in every direction. The massive machines, locked in a deadly embrace, grated to one side and came to rest half in and half out of the north ditch. Choking exhaust, steam from ruptured radiators, clouds of dust and stifling diesel fumes swirled across the wrecks. McAdie's tanker broke open and thousands of litres of fuel spewed everywhere. The pup-trailer he had been hauling ruptured on the road.

Bob Hunter was crushed in his cab, his hands still clutching the wheel. James McAdie was alive — at least for the moment.

When the transport hit, McAdie was torn from his seat, propelled through the windshield and thrown into the roadside debris. His right leg was almost severed and the force of the impact left him in shock, half-conscious and in searing pain, lying on his side in a lake of diesel fuel.

The pickup that had been following Hunter's truck was unable to stop in time and crashed into the rear of the flour transport. All three occupants of the smaller vehicle were injured, but none seriously.

In rapid succession, cars and trucks approaching from either direction stopped, their occupants hardly believing what they saw. No other driver slammed into the wrecks, but there were several close calls as the traffic ground to a halt. Within minutes several motorists rushed to the crash site. It was obvious there would be people in trouble. They assisted the occupants of the pickup truck, making sure they were in reasonable shape, then went to look for the transport drivers.

Jim McAdie was found right away, but when the onlookers saw his plight, they backed off. His mangled leg shocked some people, but even more alarming was his precarious position on the shoulder of the road. The trucker lay on a tiny ridge between the edge of the pavement and the ditch. He seemed dazed, as if he was not sure what had happened. He was surrounded by diesel fuel. Most who saw it understood, instinctively, that the slightest spark would cause the liquid to ignite — and if it did, the poor man on the ground was doomed.

McAdie cried out in pain as the diesel fuel flowed around him. Someone pleaded with him to drag himself to safety, but he obviously could not move. He had to have help. Yet in all the growing crowd of curious onlookers, pressing in and jostling for position, no one did anything. No one knew what to do.

Then Ken Bishop arrived.

When he saw that he could not drive around the

accident scene, Bishop stepped from his car and ran up the highway toward the crash site. Like all the others, he was curious about what had happened. When he did manage to thread his way through the onlookers to the front of the crowd, he was appalled at what he saw. Several people were milling around, looking confused, but no one was going to the assistance of a man lying on the shoulder of the road. Then Bishop saw the torrent of diesel fuel washing down from one of the trucks, and understood why.

Bishop could not stand where he was and do nothing. He yelled for the people to move back, then sloshed through the ankle-deep pool of fuel — toward the man he had recognized as Jim McAdie.

Because they shared the same occupation, the two had seen each other at truck stops and occasionally had coffee together. "But even if I hadn't known him," Bishop recalls, "I knew I couldn't just stand there and let him die. I had to help."

Once he reached the trucker, Bishop quickly placed a tourniquet on the injured man's leg, then raced around to the front of the transport to see if he could locate its driver. When he saw no one he frantically tore through the wreckage, silently hoping anyone in the cab would be alive.

At that point, a bystander lit a cigarette.

What McAdie remembers as "a big shot of fire" exploded around him. A column of burning fuel shot into the sky and a boom like a thunderclap shook the ground. McAdie ducked his head, prayed as he had never prayed before, and prepared to die.

The shattering blast hit Ken Bishop with the

After a bystander lit a cigarette, a huge explosion sent Bishop flying into the air, his oil-spattered clothes on fire.

impact of an express train. He was hurled into the air and thrown nine metres away, over McAdie into the deep snow near the railway line. His oil-spattered clothes were burning, obscuring his vision and searing his hair and eyebrows.

Bishop immediately rolled around in the snow, doused the flames and looked for the man he meant to save. Over by the trucks, McAdie was cloaked by dense black smoke that seemed to be everywhere. But he screamed for help, and Bishop, one arm over his face to shield it from the flames, stumbled toward the spot where McAdie lay.

The roaring fire and smoke made it hard to see, but Bishop persevered. He eventually reached the injured trucker, and then, slowly, laboriously, painfully, he managed to drag the man from danger.

Now Bishop was badly burned and near exhaustion. "All my clothes except my belt and my boots were burned off," he says. "I was barely alive." Yet despite his pleas, no one in the crowd still looking on came forward to help. Bishop's smouldering clothes were hanging from his frame and his face and hands were blackened from the fire. More than forty percent of his body had been burned. Again and again he begged for help, until finally three women produced a blanket that he pulled around his shoulders.

By this time, the Royal Canadian Mounted Police detachment in Vegreville had received a call about the accident and were on their way. But Bishop couldn't wait. Trembling with rage and pain, he made his way to his own car and managed to load McAdie into it for the trip to St. Joseph's General Hospital in Vegreville. Bishop had to do the driving himself, but before reaching the hospital he passed out. A second driver eventually completed the journey.

* * *

Ken Bishop spent eighteen days in hospitals in Vegreville and Edmonton while his burns healed. He was off work for three years because he risked his life to save another human being from certain death.

Despite Bishop's pleas for help, no one came to his aid. He had to drive the man he had saved to the hospital, alone.

James McAdie eventually recovered.

On April 5, 1976, Ken Bishop was awarded the Cross of Valour for the selfless courage of his daring rescue.

And the unthinking bystander who lit that fateful cigarette? The person slipped away into the crowd.

Jean Swedberg

Through Flames and Darkness

The town of Merritt in the British Columbia interior is nestled in a valley and surrounded on all sides by rolling, pine-studded hills that seem to go on forever. The valley is called the Nicola, after a Salish chief of long ago. Merritt was originally called The Forks, but when the railway came in 1906 the settlement was renamed Merritt to honour one of the railway promoters.

To the south of the town, high on a hill above the valley, is a lookout from which it is possible to see the entire town spread out below. One can stop at the spot and try to picture what it must have been like in earlier times, before there was a town, then later on as settlers arrived. Or you can imagine what it must have been like on the night of Wednesday, September 4, 1974, the night the Valnicola Hotel burned to the ground.

The blaze could be seen from almost anywhere in the valley. Because the fire was in the early evening, at the end of a long, beautiful day, many people were out of doors, and a crowd of 2,000 gathered to watch as the hotel was destroyed.

Among them was a young man named Dean Swedberg, who had a deeply personal reason for being there. He stood on the pavement staring into the flickering flames with an aching heart, knowing that his dear mother was dying in the inferno in front of him.

"I lived only a short distance from the hotel," he recalls, "and every night I would phone there and talk to my mother. That night when I called no one answered, even though I let the phone ring and ring. I decided to go over to the hotel and see what was wrong. But long before I got there, I expected the worst.

"I asked everybody I knew if they had seen my mother. I guess no one had, but they didn't want to come right out and tell me. Different ones would say, 'Oh yes, I think I saw her at such and such a place.' Then someone else would say they thought she was somewhere else.

"It was a hard thing waiting there so long, but by the middle of the night I knew. I waited until morning, until her body was found. Then I went home. By that time it was all over. My mother was gone."

Jean Parker Cunningham was born in Tarbalton, Scotland, on July 21, 1924. As the third youngest in a family of eleven, she was raised to believe that independence was a virtue, that being a burden to others was unacceptable. As soon as she was old enough, she enlisted in the air force. The Second World War was underway at the time, and scores of strangers in uniform were everywhere. One of them was a handsome, fair-haired young man who wore the blue serge of the Royal Canadian Air Force. His name was Stan Swedberg.

The quiet, studious, rather reserved Canadian and the young Scottish woman spent more and more time in each other's company. Finally, Stan and Jean decided to get married. The wedding took place in Scotland in 1945. One year later the newlyweds came to Canada.

The couple settled in Manitoba and started a family. Some years later, Stan and Jean and their five daughters and two sons moved to British Columbia, where Stan obtained employment on construction projects in and around Merritt. As time passed and the family grew older, Jean began to feel as though she needed to get out of the house.

She had always been active in civic organizations, particularly in the Eastern Star, and she loved to play bingo — sometimes as often as three and four times in a week. Because she had never driven a car, she looked for a part-time job that was within walking distance of her home. She found one at the thirty-two-room Valnicola Hotel.

The Valnicola was only thirteen years old. It was a two-storey frame structure with a coffee shop, dining room, lobby and lounge running across the front, facing onto Voght Street, the main thoroughfare to the east. At the back, ten bedrooms ran the length of the ground floor, while twenty more were located on the second storey. Much of the interior of the hotel was constructed of knotty pine, varnished to a shiny lustre.

"It was a combination of the wood and the varnish that caused the building to burn so rapidly," says Jack Egan, one of the owners. "I was in Vancouver the night the hotel was destroyed, but the firemen told me how quickly it went up. By the

The fire completely destroyed the Valnicola Hotel.

time I was called and I drove back here, it was all over."

On the evening of the fire, Jean Swedberg arrived at the hotel and began her duties as night clerk, looking after the front desk, answering the telephone and responding to requests from overnight guests.

One of those guests was a young man who occupied Room 9 on the ground floor at the rear of the hotel. He had a pizza delivered at around 8:00 P.M.; some time after that he lit a fire under the bed, then escaped through a back window. Later it was learned that the young man had come to Merritt to try out for a local hockey team. Because he was cut from the team he decided to vent his frustration by setting the hotel on fire. A day or so after the fire, Royal Canadian Mounted Police and officials from the fire marshal's office were able to trace the young man through the pizza delivery. He was arrested.

The fire was first noticed by Jacqui Gerow, another employee at the Valnicola. Initially the blaze seemed insignificant, and Ms. Gerow and one or two others who came to her assistance felt they could extinguish the flames themselves. They tried to do so, but within seconds the fire flared up, the bedclothes and curtains ignited and suddenly the room was in flames.

Gerow ran to call the fire department while Jean Swedberg and others went to the restaurant and lounge to tell the patrons in those rooms to flee. At first no one hurried to move, apparently because they could neither see any fire nor smell any smoke, and because there did not appear to be any immediate danger.

But Jean Swedberg knew differently. Leaving others to convince the lounge customers to leave, she rushed into the ground floor residential area of the hotel and raced from room to room, pounding on doors and shepherding occupants from the building.

As she did so, the crackling of flames could be heard in the hallway behind her. Room 9 was gutted in seconds. Billowing smoke poured from it. Already the doorjambs and walls outside the room were ablaze. Guests who came to their doors had only to glance past Jean to understand the need for urgency. One or two attempted to grab belongings, but most dropped everything and raced for the nearest exit.

The flames spread rapidly in the hallway, consuming everything as they moved. Within seconds, dense grey-black smoke made it impossible to see more than a few paces, yet Jean Swedberg continued, her eyes stinging and her lungs screaming for air.

Finally, the last guest on the ground floor was safe.

By this time, all of the coffee shop and lounge patrons were outside as well, and the first fire siren was shrieking into the night. Volunteer firefighters left whatever they were doing and hastened to help, while RCMP officers, both on duty and off, converged on the Valnicola. As the crowds gathered, a traffic jam built up in front of the hotel.

In the meantime, Dean Swedberg's phone calls to his mother went unanswered.

People who were there that night remember seeing her rush from the ground floor hallway, past the ringing telephone to the fresh air near the front doors. Then, after catching her breath and rubbing her stinging eyes, she turned back and went up the stairs that led from the lobby to the second floor bedrooms. She knew there were several occupants in those rooms, because she had seen most of them when they checked in earlier in the day. Now, as she fought her way up the stairs, a few terrified guests were coming down.

When Jean Swedberg finally reached the top of the stairs, she turned to the right and groped her way from room to room, pounding on each door and shouting for everyone to leave. Already the hallway smoke was starting to seep into many of the rooms, so guests who had been undecided about what to do had their minds made up for them.

The billowing smoke obliterated everything,

including the hallway lights, which were still functioning. But after five years at the Valnicola, Jean Swedberg knew not only how many rooms there were on either side of the stairway, but also the precise location of the rooms and exactly who was in each. No sooner had she succeeded in getting everyone out of the rooms on one end of the floor than she turned and moved as quickly as possible in the opposite direction.

Jean feared that a man in the last room on her right might be trapped. Almost by instinct, she felt her way toward his room, coughing and trying to ignore the pain in her eyes and throat. By now the smoke was black.

Out on Voght Street the first firetruck was in place, and harried firefighters were connecting hoses to the nearest hydrant. Dense clouds of smoke and sickly red-orange flames poured from the central portion of the building, as the bright neon sign in front of the hotel gleamed ghoulishly in the night. On all sides gawking crowds watched the inferno and hampered the efforts of the police, who were attempting to move the sightseers out of danger.

Gordon Sykes, one of the hotel owners, was on the scene almost from the beginning. He later told reporters that his building was consumed so quickly almost nothing was saved from it. He tried to get into Room 9 to make sure no one was trapped there, but was driven back by the flames. Some of the first police officers and firefighters also attempted to check for missing patrons, but they too were forced out.

In the meantime, Jean Swedberg was frantically

Jean Swedberg never knew that the occupant of the room she was so desperately fighting to reach had already escaped the flames.

making her way through the blackness toward the last room. Behind her, flames were roaring up the staircase, and there was no hope of turning back. Nevertheless she stumbled along, fighting to get her breath. Then, just as she reached the room she was seeking, she choked on the terrible smoke and fell to the hallway floor.

Late the next morning her body was found in the charred rubble, directly below where that last room had been. She never knew that the occupant of the room she was so desperately fighting to reach had already sensed the danger and escaped through an upper window.

One other person died in that fire, a man named Harry Navokshanoff, who may have become trapped after returning to his room to retrieve some belongings. Jack Egan credits Jean Swedberg with the rescue of at least twelve people.

"She was truly a delightful person," he recalls. "She had such a bubbling personality that it was almost impossible to be depressed when she was around.

"Jean enjoyed her work and loved meeting people. She was also totally reliable," he says. "She was working at the hotel when I bought the place, so I didn't hire her. But I kept her on because she was so good at her job."

She was also a true hero, a woman with depths of courage no one had imagined.

Mary Dohey

Hijacked!

The big Air Canada jet lumbered out to the runway, received clearance for takeoff, and roared into the sky at precisely 4:15 P.M. Below and behind, Calgary looked like a toy town on the edge of the Alberta prairie. Tiny trucks raced along tiny roads, and the dots that had been cars disappeared. For a time the mountains were visible, but soon even they were gone. Within minutes Flight 812, bound for Toronto and Montreal, reached its cruising altitude.

One of the passengers on that plane was twenty-seven-year-old Paul Joseph Cini. For the past seven years his life had been a litany of failures, both personal and professional. He had been, among other things, a soldier, a car thief and a truck driver. He had a son, but saw him only once before the baby's mother put him up for adoption soon after he was born.

Paul Cini had spent the past summer and early autumn drinking and acquiring some strange paraphernalia: a black balaclava, a wig, some dynamite, a shotgun and a parachute. The inadequacies of his life had been bothering Cini. He felt he had to do something, anything, in order to prove to himself and to the whole world that he was important. He decided to hijack a plane.

On November 12, 1971, he boarded Air Canada's Flight 812. His plan was to take over the plane, collect a ransom and then parachute from the aircraft and disappear without a trace. He had everything he needed under his long, oversized beige trench coat and in the shopping bag he carried. But he had not counted on meeting someone like Mary Dohey.

Mary Dohey was a flight attendant on the plane Cini picked to hijack. She had suffered as much as, perhaps more than, Cini, but had risen above it. She had been orphaned when she was only three, and in the years after moved around to several foster homes. She was abused in some, lonely in most, but unbelievably resilient in them all. She put herself through school, and for a time became a teacher in Newfoundland. When she realized that a career in teaching was not what she wanted, she went back to her studies and obtained her Registered Nurse's certificate, specializing in psychiatry.

Next Mary Dohey began looking for a career in the air. She longed to travel, and the idea of getting paid to do so was appealing. Air Canada, or Trans-Canada Airlines, as the company was formerly known, was looking for flight attendants. Dohey was accepted.

"I have enjoyed this life," she says, "but of all the flying I've done, the night of the hijacking was something I will never forget. If I live to be a million, I will never get over that nightmare."

The nightmare began less than an hour out of

Calgary. The passenger sitting in seat 2B — first class — bolted down a vodka and orange juice and then left his seat to go to a washroom at the front of the plane. Five minutes later John Arpin, the forty-eight-year-old purser on the flight, heard a noise behind him. He turned and looked straight into the muzzle of a sawed-off double-barrelled shotgun. On the other end of it was a grotesque-looking figure in a trench coat, black balaclava and black wig, sitting at a small table in the otherwise empty first-class lounge.

"Sit over here," roared a male voice from under the black hood.

Arpin sat down.

"Take this and show it to the captain, and tell him to follow these instructions to a T," ordered the man.

He handed Arpin a sheet of yellow paper. The purser started to read.

"That's for the captain, not you!" shrieked the man, jamming the gun into Arpin's face.

At that point, Mary Dohey walked into the lounge. She was about to speak to Arpin when she saw the gun.

"Sit down," demanded the figure in the black hood.

"Sit down, Mary," said Arpin. "It's for real."

As Mary took a seat beside the purser, the man in the mask swung the shotgun over to her and placed both barrels up against her forehead.

"Now take that note to the captain," he said to Arpin, "and be quick about it. If you are not back right away, I'm killing your stewardess. Now *you*," he said, referring to Mary, "get over there by the window. Stand with your back against it and stare straight ahead. If you move, I'll blow your head off."

Mary Dohey went over to the window and Arpin disappeared into the cockpit. There he handed Captain Vern Ehman, a forty-three-year-old pilot from Montreal, the sheet of yellow paper. On it was a 506-word message that began with "Welcome aboard the original doomsday flight" and ended with "There'll be no heroes tonight, for tonight we all will die." The note demanded a ransom of $1.5 million and instructed the captain to fly to Great Falls, Montana. The money was to be collected there, and according to the note, had to be delivered to the plane by a woman.

While Arpin was on the flight deck delivering the note, the hijacker produced a sixty-stick dynamite bomb. He handed Mary two wires protruding from it and told her to hold them apart. "If you don't," he snarled, "these wires will complete a circuit and this bomb will explode. If you want to die right now, you can let them touch." With that, he ordered her to sit beside him, with her back against the side of the plane. "Stare straight ahead," he repeated.

"I did exactly as he told me," Mary Dohey recalls. "I had one wire beside my little finger and another by my thumb, and I held them that way for over four hours. But my God, I was terrified, so terrified. I had to keep staring ahead, so I looked across to a window at the other side. I knew the awful situation we were in, and I thought I would likely be dead before Johnny Arpin got back from the cockpit. All this time I was praying, praying harder than I'd ever prayed before."

As the seconds ticked away and Arpin still had

not returned, the man with the shotgun became more and more agitated.

"I could see his eyes through the slits in the black hood," Dohey says with a shiver, "and I could tell he was pretty jumpy. Then I noticed that his trigger finger was trembling.

"When I saw that, I was sure I was dead, so I made my peace with God. I was prepared to die. Then suddenly the gun started waving around and it went off."

"It was a terrible, terrible nightmare. I really expected we were all going to die."

Today Mary grimaces as she recalls the terrifying incident.

"The barrel was right beside my ear when the shot was fired," she says. "My head was ringing from the sound as the shot went into a wall."

The blast thudded into the cockpit bulkhead and tore a fist-sized hole through it. Spent pellets, dust and debris showered down on the second officer, and John Arpin was sure Mary Dohey was dead. He hurried back to the lounge.

As he did he heard the hijacker say to Mary, "I'm sorry, I didn't mean to do that."

She took up the cue. "I know you didn't, dear. You don't want to hurt us, do you?" Her soft voice and sympathetic manner confused Paul Cini. She began to talk to him, hoping to gain his confidence. "My name is Mary," she said.

"Is that really your name?" Cini asked.

"Yes, it is," she answered. "Do you like it?"

"Yes, it's a nice name."

"Well, then, you may call me Mary. What is your name?"

"It's Dennis," lied Cini.

"Okay, Dennis," said the stewardess, "may I hold your hand?" With that she took the hijacker's hand in hers, all the while talking to him in a gentle, caring tone.

"I talked to him as I have never talked to anyone before or since," she recalls. "I asked him about himself and I told him about me. We covered almost every topic I could think of, from the weather to sports, to jobs, to children. When I told him I was the youngest of fourteen children, he laughed and told me that was a lot of kids. I knew then that he liked children, and I told myself that fact might be something I could use later on. I was trying to find anything I could to calm the guy. The talking was so hard, though. The saliva in my mouth kept drying up, I was so scared."

When Arpin returned from the flight deck, Cini demanded to know if the captain understood the message.

"Yes," answered Arpin. "We're to go to Montana, pick up the money, then go to Regina, release the passengers, load the aircraft full of guns and ammunition, and head for Ireland."

"That's right," Cini agreed.

"But where does the money come from?" Arpin asked.

"Air Canada supplies the money," Cini yelled. "Go and tell the captain that."

Arpin returned to the cockpit with the message. He also told Captain Ehman that the hijacker's name was Dennis and that the stewardess was sitting beside him, holding his hand and trying to calm him down.

"Good," replied the pilot. "Keep me posted." With that he radioed Winnipeg ground control and passed on the new instructions. Already the plane had been in the air for more than an hour.

During the flight into the United States, Cini would flare up at a moment's notice. Just when Mary began to feel that things might get better, they got worse. The hijacker complained of the heat in the plane, so the temperature was lowered. Arpin asked if he could put his coat on, but when he did, Cini saw the gold braid around the cuffs of the jacket and accused Arpin of being with the Federal Bureau of Investigation. When Arpin was asked about his nationality and said he was French, Cini shrieked, "It's good that you're not English, because I'm going to kill every Englishman on this plane."

Because the shotgun blast was loud enough to be heard by the passengers, Arpin asked Cini how the noise should be explained to them.

"Tell them a light bulb blew," the hijacker snapped. "Tell them whatever you want."

Arpin walked back to the first-class section and informed the passengers of the hijacking. "And if our guest comes back here," he warned, "don't let on that any of you are English. He told us he would kill anyone who was English."

Most of the passengers remained calm, although two got up and ran down the aisle toward the back of the plane. A few asked for drinks.

Shortly after Arpin returned to the lounge, assistant purser Philip Bonné entered. Up to that point, he did not know of the hijacking, nor did most of the passengers in the economy section at the rear of the plane. Cini ordered Bonné to sit down beside Arpin.

"What nationality are you?" Cini asked him.

"I'm French Canadian."

"Well then, I'll blow your head off. The FLQ would be proud of me and DeGaulle would turn over in his grave."

No one knew what this meant.

A few seconds later Cini reached into the pocket of his trench coat and pulled out two bundles of dynamite. There were five sticks in each bundle.

"Now I'm going to light these fuses and blow up the plane," he said.

Mary Dohey turned to him. "But Dennis, why would you do that, dear? You're going to hurt a lot of people. Do you know those people?"

Cini changed his mind. Instead, he took one stick of dynamite and pushed it into John Arpin's mouth. He then aimed the shotgun at Arpin's head.

Again Mary interceded. "Dennis, dear," she whispered, "why don't you put the safety catch on the gun?"

Cini became confused.

"Sit over there," he roared at Bonné. The assistant purser moved to the seat across the table from Dohey. "Now take her hands," Cini demanded.

Bonné did so.

"Hold her hands so tight I can see the whites of your knuckles," Cini snapped.

While this was happening, John Arpin slowly withdrew the dynamite from his mouth. Cini saw him and jammed the explosive back in again. Then he apparently changed his mind, grabbed the dynamite and ordered Mary Dohey to smell it.

"My darling, I don't know anything about dynamite," she protested.

Cini set the stick on the table.

By this time, the plane had reached Great Falls, but Cini ordered it to circle the airport until the money he had demanded was ready. As soon as Captain Ehman received a radio message that the money was at the airport, he landed the DC-8. A police secretary walked out to the plane and tied the suitcase she carried onto a leather strap Bonné lowered from the aircraft. Bonné hauled the case containing the money into the plane and Ehman took off again. Fifteen minutes had passed.

As soon as the jet was at its cruising altitude, Cini ordered Arpin to count the money. As he did so he realized, to his horror, that the suitcase contained only $50,000, not the $1.5 million Cini had demanded. Fortunately the hijacker did not notice the discrepancy.

"By this time, I realized just how mad the whole

escapade was," recalls Mary. "It was a terrible, terrible nightmare, and I really expected we were all going to die. I made a pact with God at that time," she continues. "I told Him I would gladly die, but He had to show me a way to save the passengers. Then I recalled that the hijacker had seemed pleased when I told him I came from a family of fourteen, that he seemed to like kids."

Mary turned to Cini. "Dennis, I hear the children crying," she said.

"Do you mean there are *kids* on here?" Cini asked, apparently dumbfounded that could be so.

"Oh yes," she said, "and I can hear them crying. The dear little things are so tired and hungry. They don't know what's happening."

Cini reacted in fury.

"Go up and tell that captain," he said to Arpin, "to go back to Great Falls and let the people off. I am going to need the space for the ammunition."

Ehman swung the plane around and returned to Great Falls. The 118 passengers began leaving.

"Now," Cini barked at Arpin, "I have a blue suitcase on this plane. I want you to get it — now! I'll give you ten minutes, and if you are not back with it then, I am going to kill this stewardess." He handed Arpin a baggage tag and checked his watch. Arpin scrambled down the ramp.

As soon as the purser had gone, Cini ordered Mary to turn around. Then he placed the muzzle of the shotgun against the back of her neck. She knew he was watching the time.

"Those minutes were some of the worst of my entire life," she says. "I could feel the cold steel on my neck and I really thought I would be killed —

The hijacked jetliner surrounded by lights at the Calgary Airport.

particularly when Johnny was delayed."

"Well, your time is up," Cini told her. Then he cocked the hammer of the gun. Mary asked if she could turn around. Cini consented.

"When I turned, he put the gun up against my forehead. But that was better than behind me, because I didn't think he could face me and kill me. I started pleading for him to give Johnny a bit more time. I told him how hard it would be to find one suitcase among all the others."

Just as Arpin returned, and after the last passenger was off, Cini leaned close to Mary and whispered, "Do you want to leave? If you want to leave, you can go."

Dohey was momentarily stunned by the sudden turn of events, but then she realized that if she left, the hijacker would blow up the plane. "I was worried about the pilot and the rest of the crew," she says. "I knew I had to fight to save them. By this time, I had developed some rapport with the hijacker and I knew that if I could not control him, we would all die."

"Do you want me to leave, dear?" Dohey asked.

"No, I want you to stay," muttered Cini.

"Then if you want me to stay, I'll stay."

"You're a fool for not going," Arpin told her as the plane left Great Falls for the second time that evening. "You should have left when you had the chance."

When the aircraft was well underway, this time toward Phoenix, Arizona, and not Regina as he had demanded earlier, Cini again changed his mind. He told Arpin to let the captain know they should fly to Calgary. Ehman agreed.

Then the already volatile hijacker became even more worked up. At one point he accused the crew of piping lethal gas into the plane to kill him. On another occasion he flew into a rage because he lit a cigarette and found that it was not his own brand. To ensure that this did not happen again, he ordered Dohey, Arpin and Bonné to sit down with him at the little table in the lounge.

When all four were seated, he took one cigarette from each of four packs, all different brands. He ordered Mary to light each and set them in an ashtray in the centre of the table. Then he turned the ashtray around and around, all the while telling his hostages that if the cigarette he selected from the ashtray was not his own, Mary would die.

He picked the right one and Mary Dohey almost collapsed with relief. "By this time, I was so tired, I almost gave up," she recalls.

As the big jet flew north, Cini embarked on yet another mad endeavour. He suddenly sprang to his feet and rushed into the cockpit.

"The next thing I knew," Dohey says, "he came marching out of the cockpit, behind the captain, with the shotgun aimed at the back of Vern's head. The captain was carrying all the radio headsets."

The two went down the centre aisle of the plane, back toward the now empty economy section. When they reached the tail section, Cini told Ehman to open a door there, because he wanted to parachute out. Ehman refused, saying that opening the door would be impossible because of the slipstream. "Then I'll blow the back off the plane and jump out," Cini retorted.

Ehman dissuaded him, pointing out that if he really wanted to jump out, he could leave through one of the emergency windows. Cini agreed, but found that he could not open the window with one hand. When he set the shotgun down in order to free both his hands, Ehman saw his chance.

The pilot grabbed the shotgun and heaved it down the aisle. Then he lunged for Cini's throat, and at the same time yelled for help.

John Arpin raced to assist. Then Bonné and Dohey arrived. The four of them pinned Cini to the floor and he stopped struggling.

"We've got to tie him up," Ehman said, "Get some tape."

Suddenly Cini went berserk. He threw them off and began to thrash around like a wild animal. Ehman grabbed the man's throat and the others fought to control him. They threw him down, but again he clambered to his feet.

"The axe, Phillip!" Ehman yelled. "Hit him with the axe."

Phillip Bonné grabbed an emergency fire axe and belted Cini on the head with the blunt end. Cini shook off the blow and lunged at the captain. Bonné clouted him with the blade. Blood flew, but Cini was as ferocious as ever.

"Use the handle," yelled Ehman.

Bonné flipped the axe around, took the blade in both hands and brought the handle down.

There was a crunching sound, and the hijacker's body went limp. Arpin pulled off the hood Cini wore and they tied him down. Captain Ehman returned to the cockpit. Half an hour later he brought Flight 812 down on the tarmac at Calgary — just twenty minutes before a heavy fog closed the airport for two days. It was now midnight, but the terrible ordeal was over.

* * *

After he had recovered from his head wounds, Paul Joseph Cini was sent to prison. John Arpin, Vern Ehman, Phillip Bonné and Mary Dohey were all decorated for bravery, but Dohey alone received the Cross of Valour. She was the first person to earn the award without having died to earn it. And she returned to flying.

Partanen and Stringer

Explosion at Sea!

The sea was calm at first light, yet slate-grey and cold. Leaden clouds touched the horizon and the mist of morning wrapped the ship like a shroud. Across her clammy decks, rivulets of water drained into shallow pools which reflected the dismal sky. Behind lay the coast of England, while ahead, an ocean away, was Canada. The ship had been away for weeks, and as always, the crew longed to return home. Another few days and they would be there — or at least, most of them would be there.

The ship was called the *Kootenay,* a destroyer with 225 officers and crew on board. On this morning of October 23, 1969, she and eight other Canadian Navy ships were westbound out of the English Channel.

"We had just finished over six weeks of exercises and we were finally on our way home," recalls Mike Aris, a senior able seaman in the sonar branch. "All we wanted to do was stand our watches, relax a bit and go home. I had just been married in August of that year and this trip had begun in early September, so I was looking forward to its end. A lot of the guys felt the same way I did."

One of the ships with the *Kootenay* that morning was the *Saguenay*. Both had been ordered to break away from the rest of the formation in order to conduct full-power drills, trial runs at speeds in excess of twenty-eight knots. The aircraft carrier *Bonaventure* and the rest of the task group were not involved. In fact, at the time the *Kootenay* began her drills, all of the other ships in the area were over the horizon.

Between 6:00 and 7:00 A.M., the *Kootenay* maintained an even twenty-five knots. Her speed was then gradually increased until 8:10, when the order "Full speed ahead, both engines" was given. The ship was running well and, despite the dullness of the morning, its speed made spirits rise.

At precisely 8:16 Lieutenant Al Kennedy, the ship's engineer, entered the engine room after having visited the boiler room. As he walked through he spoke to the men and felt the two main engine gear boxes. While both were quite warm, he had no trouble bearing the heat with the palm of his hand. He nodded at John MacKinnon and Eric Harman, who were at the throttles, and then stopped to talk with Chief Petty Officer Vaino "Ski" Partanen.

It was the last conversation Partanen would ever have.

Suddenly a sound, which would later be described by some as like the hiss of a welding torch, and by others as like a crash, erupted in the engine room. The starboard gearcase exploded, driving deadly shards of metal across the room. The high-speed pinion bearings within the gearcase itself had become overheated, and their heat combined with

the oil vapour present in the air to cause a sponta-
neous explosion. Almost immediately the engine
room was engulfed in flames and intense heat.

One of the men, Able Seaman Mike Hardy, was
thrown from an overhead catwalk, his clothes in
flames. Lieutenant Kennedy bounded toward the
port throttle in a vain attempt to close it. One and
possibly two others in the room tried to do the same
thing with the starboard throttle.

A white-hot sheet of flame flashed across the
chamber, tore into seven crewmen who were close
at hand and killed them instantly. Three others
were able to flee the inferno. One of these, Al
Kennedy, somehow scrambled up the forward
engine room ladder and raced to the bridge to
sound the alarm.

Several men who saw him remember his soot-
blackened face and clothes. And even though he
was badly burned, with strips of flesh hanging from
his face and arms, he was still coherent when he
reached the bridge. He blurted out the situation in
the engine room and then slumped to the deck,
trembling in pain and shock. Someone gave him
morphine from the captain's safe.

Back in the flame-engulfed engine room, Ski
Partanen's thoughts were for the safety of the ship
and the officers and men on it. Although searing
flames obliterated everything around him, he
remained where he was in the engine room. Even
as he knew he was dying, he grabbed the phone to
the wheelhouse and screamed, "Request permis-
sion to stop both engines!"

The request was relayed to the bridge, and the
officer of the watch immediately ordered both

Despite flames raging through the engine room, Ski Partanen stayed at his post to warn the bridge that there had been an explosion.

engines stopped. By this time dense, acrid clouds of smoke were billowing through the ship.

"I was in the engine room a couple of seconds before the explosion," recalls Russell "Sandy" Saunders, an air force corporal on duty with the navy at the time. But Saunders had left the room to get some coffee. That decision saved his life.

"I had just climbed the ladder from the engine room," he says, "and was in the act of stepping out into what we called Burma Road, a passageway down through the centre of the ship, when I noticed a terrific wind on my back. I was lifted from my feet and propelled forward. I felt a tremendous crush as the right side of my body hit the mailbox by the cafeteria.

"Just as that was happening, somebody came out of the cafeteria and asked me what was wrong. I started to tell him, and as I did so, I looked back over my shoulder. Huge balls of fire were coming out of the afterhatch of the engine room. A figure appeared in the flames, screaming, his clothes on fire and his hands and face burned raw.

"The fireballs seemed to be alive. They bounced from one side of the hall to the other and came right down Burma Road after me. I barged into the cafeteria to get away from the flames [and saw] Sergeant Lou Stringer in the first seat. Most of the men still had their heads down over their meals because the full impact of what had happened had not sunk in. Lou was the first to react.

"He asked me what was wrong, and before I even finished answering he was on his feet beside me. He had been around a little longer than the rest of us, and I suppose that was why he sensed the danger before the others. There were no escape hatches in the cafeteria."

By this time the fire had blocked the only other exit from the cafeteria and flames began inching their way across the ceiling. The appearance of the flames set off a wild stampede for the door that Saunders had just entered.

"Suddenly every man in the room seemed to be charging me," he recalls, "but I kept shouting that there was no escape that way, that Burma Road was full of fire. Stringer told the men to get down and get something over their faces to breathe through. Then he helped me keep people from going out into the hallway.

"Just opposite where we stood was the servery, with the opening to it covered by a corrugated metal door. We started pounding on that door and finally somebody opened it to see what the racket was. As soon as the opening appeared, people began piling through it, climbing up over the steam tables in order to get out through the galley. By this time the whole place was starting to fill with smoke."

As the choking smoke poured into the cafeteria, the men became hysterical. They screamed and cried, jostling and climbing over each other in a desperate rush to escape. Some flattened themselves on the deck, breathed through clothing and prayed for rescue. Others tried to push past Saunders and Stringer, toward what would have been certain death in the hallway outside.

"If Lou hadn't been beside me, a lot of guys would have died right there," says Saunders. "The ones that were later rescued in the cafeteria owe their lives to him. And he was really responsible for getting the rest through into the galley where the cooks led them out.

"Until the day I die, I will never forget the screaming and the terrible things I saw that morning," continues Saunders with a shudder. "Men were crying, cursing and praying all at the same time. I heard somebody saying a rosary and I thought that wasn't such a bad idea, so I too cried out to God and asked Him to help me. I remember praying that I might see my wife and children again. At the time I had a son who was four years old and a daughter who had just been born, but I really thought they had seen their dad for the last time.

"The smoke became thicker and blacker, almost within seconds. It became harder and harder to breathe, and when you did breathe, the chemicals in the smoke and the heat from the fire seemed to burn right into your lungs.

"I remember losing and gaining consciousness while I was standing there. I couldn't see a thing in the black smoke, and after awhile my throat didn't hurt anymore and I wasn't able to feel anything in my arms and legs. That was when I knew I was dying. I don't remember falling."

Elsewhere on the ship, John Montague was in his bunk at the time of the engine-room explosion. He had been on watch from midnight until four that morning and had expected to sleep until about nine.

"Just after 8:20, the telephone rang in my cabin," he recalls. "When I answered I heard Sub-Lieutenant Gerry Gadd shouting, 'Get out of there. The ship's on fire.' Almost at the same instant two people burst into my cabin, coughing and gagging because of the thick, black, oily smoke. Because I was just wearing underwear shorts, I grabbed a pair of khaki trousers, but that was all the dressing I had time to do. One of the men who had come into my cabin was shouting out at someone, 'Open the hatch! Open the hatch!' in reference to the main hatch which led to the upper deck.

"The hatch was open, but the black smoke made it look as if it was closed. The man then left my cabin and made a dash down the passageway to the ladder which led to the hatchway and the exit to the upper deck.

"I told the other guy we'd better get out as well. He hesitated to leave my cabin, so I grabbed him by his belt and literally pushed him all the way down the passageway to the ladder to the upper deck. Once we were out of the smoke he was okay. Later he thanked me."

When the fire on board had started, Commander Neil Norton, captain of the *Kootenay*, was in his

148

Lou Stringer stopped men from pushing past him into what would have been certain death.

cabin. Because he was some distance from the engine room, he noticed only a slight bump at the time of the explosion. But fifteen seconds later it seemed the entire ship was filled with smoke, and he knew something was seriously wrong. Then came the announcement from the bridge: "All hands to emergency stations. Fire in the engine room. This is not a drill." With that, Norton and his executive officer raced to the bridge to take control. The ship's company were already on their way to emergency stations.

The officer of the watch at the time of the explosion was John Keenliside. He had given the order, "Full speed ahead, both engines," as well as the orders, "Stop both engines!" and "All hands to emergency stations!" Later he would tell a board of inquiry that by the time he had finished giving the emergency announcement the smoke had reached the bridge.

Back in the engine room the fire had become an inferno. The last man out, Able Seaman George

"Dinger" Bell, had been pushed up the ladder to safety by Leading Seaman Gary Hutton. Hutton did not survive. And Ski Partanen's last message was garbled, but its tone was clear. The situation was desperate. All hope had gone.

In the cafeteria, the crush of men trying to get out went at a slower and slower pace as the deadly smoke took its toll. The cafeteria was above the burning engine room and the floor was hot — so hot that in the spots immediately above the gearcases the asphalt tiles were beginning to bubble. The entire room was a shambles: dishes and food littered the floor, and the taps on two large milk urns had broken open, spewing cold milk onto the deck. But the cold milk saved those men who had collapsed on the floor from being burned alive.

"I could still hear the screams of other men," says Saunders, "but I never heard Lou [Stringer] complain. He just kept on trying to get the men out of there. He was the least likely guy to stand with his back against the wall when the chips were down. Ordinarily he was a spectator in sports and so on, but this time, when he was really needed, he stood by his men. When he was needed, he was brave in a way the others couldn't touch. I'll never forget him for that.

"After a time I somehow realized that we were lying on the floor, but I had lost all sense of direction and I could feel no pain. Then somehow through the smoke I could see light and the words 'Where there's light, there's air' kept running through my mind. I turned toward the light and kept breathing deeply in that direction. Then I heard someone ask a ridiculous question: 'Is there any-body alive down here?'

"A guy wearing a Chemox breathing apparatus was coming toward me, shining a light through the smoke. I tried to yell at him but because my throat was burned I couldn't make any sound. I did have some strength in my arms, though, and I was able to grab his leg as he went by. He half dragged, half carried me away. Finally we came to the hatchway and I remember seeing it through the smoke, cloud-ed but yet bright. Then the moment I hit the fresh air, I passed out.

"At about the same time as the fireballs were roaring down Burma Road, Mike Aris and another sailor were busy scrubbing the Number 1 mess hall near the bow of the ship. At the instant of the explo-sion, both noticed that their ears popped, but there was no other indication that anything was wrong. Then a few seconds later the action alarm sounded. The coxswain came up the ladder to the mess where we were and virtually screamed at us to get out of there. We knew from the tone of his voice that this was no exercise.

"As we started out, we had no idea where the trouble was, but when we got to Burma Road we realized how serious things were. The whole pas-sageway was full of black smoke, and it seemed to be getting thicker all the time. We proceeded as quickly as we could to what were called the ward-room flats. There was a ladder there and everyone was waiting his turn to go up. Most of the waiting was orderly, although one guy panicked and pushed some others out of the way and rushed up.

"While I was waiting I noticed a guy screaming

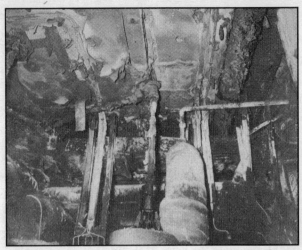

The engine room was completely gutted by the fire.

and it took me a few seconds to realize that it was Dinger Bell. I didn't recognize him at first because his skin was black and burnt and it was hanging off his face and arms. At that point I remember being really scared."

In all, more than forty minutes had elapsed since the explosion, and during much of this period the *Kootenay* was technically out of control. The ship's steering lines had burned out when the fire started, but because the boilers were still functioning, the vessel was able to continue on its way as if nothing had happened.

While all this was going on, officers on the bridge were desperately trying to find out how serious the situation was, and to call for help. But the smoke and the breakdown of communications made it almost impossible. For a time, all the radios on board were out, so none of the other vessels in the task group was aware that the *Kootenay* was in trouble. Even if one had been, the nearest was twenty-seven kilometres away.

During the time officers on the bridge were attempting to call for help, most of the ship's company was pouring out onto the deck. Mike Aris remembers:

"We reached our emergency stations, and we were all pretty nervous. We pulled our life jackets around our necks and watched the smoke pour out of the ship. At this point no one knew whether we were going to abandon her or not. I noticed one guy who couldn't swim, so I offered him my life jacket, but he refused to take it. He kept saying he wouldn't need it, that we wouldn't be leaving. I'm afraid I wasn't that confident.

"As we stood there, we heard rumours that the fire was in the boiler room, right underneath where about forty of us had collected. Somebody claimed there might be another explosion, so we all cleared out of there fast."

The deadly smoke from the engine room was still coursing through the *Kootenay* as the first rescue teams began assembling on the upper decks. Men donned Chemox breathing packs or diving masks and tanks in order to be able to function in the smoke.

"During all of this time the ship was still going ahead on the port screw," Mike Aris continues. "There was no steering capability left, so we were going in a huge lazy circle at full speed. As we stood on the quarterdeck we saw red flares being fired from the bridge, and that certainly emphasized how serious the situation was. There were still no other ships in sight, so suddenly it was very lonesome.

"But radio contact was eventually made, and I still believe the most beautiful sight I have ever seen was the *Bonaventure* and all her escorts coming over the horizon at full steam, led by a half dozen or so of her helicopters. One by one they discharged foam, firefighters and breathing equipment. Then, as one of the helicopters took away the body of a man who had died, I felt like crying."

In all, nine men lost their lives and fifty-three others were injured in the explosion and fire on the *Kootenay* that cold October morning in 1969. And while those who were there all have different memories of the accident, none of them will ever forget it.

* * *

Three years later, the Cross of Valour was awarded posthumously to both Ski Partanen and to Lou Stringer for their heroism that day. Partanen's body was found — still at his post — in the engine room, while Sergeant Stringer died two days later from the after-effects of his ordeal.

John Melady has always wondered why people push themselves to extremes. He has been fascinated by many of the people in this book, ordinary people who took extraordinary action when they could have played it safe. John feels privileged to have met many of the Cross of Valour heroes — people who took only a split second to decide to put their lives at risk to help others.

John is an adventure lover himself. He has flown in a fighter jet and a World War II bomber, parasailed, rock climbed, ridden in a hot air balloon — even hung from a harness attached to a helicopter to take pictures for one of his books.

He lives with his wife in Brighton, Ontario.

Other books by John Melady:

Explosion

Escape From Canada!

Korea: Canada's Forgotten War

The Little Princes

Overtime, Overdue: The Bill Barilko Story

Pilots

Heartbreak and Heroism: Canadian Search and Rescue Stories

Cover photograph: Greg Latza/Photographic Arts & Illustration NETwork.

The author gratefully acknowledges all those who have provided photographs for this book. Particular credit is given to the following: Correctional Service Canada (84), Department of National Defence Canada (152), John Evans Photo (100 and insert on cover), Glenbow Archives (138), Government House, Ottawa (40), Stu LeBaron (96), Livingston Photo (67), *Merritt Herald* (122), Royal Canadian Mounted Police (52).